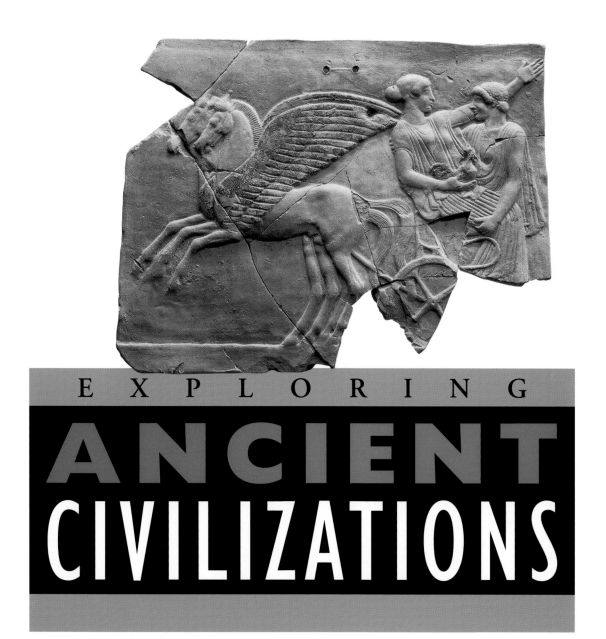

EXPLORING
ANCIENT
CIVILIZATIONS

5

Greece – Indian Philosophy

Marshall Cavendish

Sydney

Marshall Cavendish
99 White Plains Road
Tarrytown, New York 10591-9001

www.marshallcavendish.com

Consultants: Daud Ali, School of Oriental and African
Studies, University of London; Michael Brett, School
of Oriental and African Studies, London; John
Chinnery, School of Oriental and African Studies,
London; Philip de Souza; Joann Fletcher; Anthony
Green; Peter Groff, Department of Philosophy,
Bucknell University; Mark Handley, History
Department, University College London; Anders
Karlsson, School of Oriental and African Studies,
London; Alan Leslie, Glasgow University Archaeology
Research Department; Michael E. Smith, Department
of Anthropology, University at Albany; Matthew
Spriggs, Head of School of Archaeology and
Anthropology, Australian National University

Contributing authors: Richard Balkwill, Richard
Burrows, Peter Chrisp, Richard Dargie, Steve Eddy,
Clive Gifford, Jen Green, Peter Hicks, Robert Hull,
Jonathan Ingoldby, Pat Levy, Steven Maddocks, John
Malam, Saviour Pirotta, Stewart Ross, Sean Sheehan,
Jane Shuter

WHITE-THOMSON PUBLISHING
Editor: Alex Woolf
Design: Derek Lee
Cartographer: Peter Bull Design
Picture Research: Glass Onion Pictures
Indexer: Fiona Barr

MARSHALL CAVENDISH
Editor: Thomas McCarthy
Editorial Director: Paul Bernabeo
Production Manager: Michael Esposito

Library of Congress Cataloging-in-Publication Data
Exploring ancient civilizations.
    p. cm.
Includes bibliographical references and indexes.
  ISBN 0-7614-7456-0 (set : alk. paper) -- ISBN 0-7614-7457-9 (v. 1 :
alk. paper) -- ISBN 0-7614-7458-7 (v. 2 : alk. paper) -- ISBN
0-7614-7459-5 (v. 3 : alk. paper) -- ISBN 0-7614-7460-9 (v. 4 : alk.
paper) -- ISBN 0-7614-7461-7 (v. 5 : alk. paper) -- ISBN 0-7614-7462-5
(v. 6 : alk. paper) -- ISBN 0-7614-7463-3 (v. 7 : alk. paper) -- ISBN
0-7614-7464-1 (v. 8 : alk. paper) -- ISBN 0-7614-7465-X (v. 9 : alk.
paper) -- ISBN 0-7614-7466-8 (v. 10 : alk. paper) -- ISBN 0-7614-7467-6
(v. 11 : alk. paper)
  1. Civilization, Ancient--Encyclopedias.
 CB311.E97 2004
 930'.03--dc21

                                    2003041224

ISBN 0-7614-7456-0 (set)
ISBN 0-7614-7461-7 (vol. 5)

Printed and bound in China

07 06 05 04 03 5 4 3 2 1

ILLUSTRATION CREDITS

AKG London: 325 (John Hios), 326 (Erich Lessing / National Archaeological Museum,
Athens), 327 (Erich Lessing / Musée du Louvre, Paris), 329 (Erich Lessing / Musée du
Louvre, Paris), 330 (Erich Lessing / Musée du Louvre, Paris), 332 (Erich Lessing / Pergamon
Museum, Berlin), 333 (Erich Lessing / Museo Archeologico Nazionale, Aquileia, Italy), 334
(Museo Nazionale Archeologico di Reggio Calabria, Italy), 335 (Erich Lessing / Musée du
Louvre, Paris), 339, 349 (Erich Lessing), 354, 359 (Erich Lessing / Israel Museum,
Jerusalem), 366 (Jean-Louis Nou), 370 (Erich Lessing / Oriental Museum, Istanbul), 382,
385 (McGregor Museum, Kimberley, South Africa), 386 (Sousse Archaeological Museum,
Tunisia), 390 (Keith Collie), 393 (Erich Lessing / Bibliothèque Nationale, Paris), 397 (British
Library), 398 (Jean-Louis Nou / Prince of Wales Museum, Bombay).
Art Archive / Dagli Orti: 360, 361, 363, 369, 375, 376 (Musée Cernuschi, Paris), 377
(British Museum, London), 378 (Archaeological Museum, Naples), 383, 387.
Bridgeman Art Library: 328 (British Museum, London), 330 (Museo Archeologico
Nazionale, Naples), 331 (Hermitage Museum, St. Petersburg, Russia), 336, 337 (Charles
Plante Fine Arts), 338 (British Museum, London), 343 (Museo Archeologico Nazionale,
Naples), 344, 346 (Visual Arts Library, London), 347 (Museo Archeologico Nazionale,
Naples), 350, 351 (British Museum, London), 352 (Verulamium Museum, St. Albans, UK),
353 (British Museum, London), 356 (Museo di San Marco dell'Angelico, Florence), 357
(Vatican Museums and Galleries), 358, 364 (Ann & Bury Peerless Picture Library), 365 (Ann
& Bury Peerless Picture Library), 367 (Giraudon / Lauros), 380 (British Museum, London),
383 (Vatican Museums and Galleries), 392 (Museo Capitolino, Rome), 395 (India Office
Library, London), 396 (British Library, London).
British Library: 379.
Werner Forman Archive: 342 (Theresa McCullough Collection, London), 371 (Schimmel
Collection, New York), 373 (Peabody Museum, Harvard University), 374 (Smithsonian
Institution, Washington, DC), 388 (Edgar Knobloch), 394 (British Museum, London).

Contents

Greece, Classical

Greece is located in the northeastern section of the Mediterranean Sea. The classical period in Greece began around 500 BCE. During the following one hundred years, Greek culture flourished, especially in the city-state of Athens, and Greek ideas and discoveries produced art, architecture, drama, science, and philosophy that were to form the foundation of later Western civilization.

The earliest recognizably Greek civilization, the Mycenaean, flourished between 1600 and 1200 BCE. When the Mycenaean Age came to an end, around the twelfth century BCE, there followed a period, lasting until about 800 BCE, known as the Dark Ages, when the art of writing was lost. Toward 800 BCE the Greeks began to use writing again. Around 700 BCE Homer, Greece's greatest poet, composed the *Iliad* and the *Odyssey*. During the next two centuries the Greeks made steady advances in economic, political, and cultural matters.

Between 490 and 479 BCE, the Greek city-states joined forces to fight off the might of the Persian Empire. The city-states also fought with each other. Toward the end of the century, Athens was defeated by Sparta, another powerful city-state, in the Peloponnesian War (431–404 BCE). The classical period ended in around 336 BCE, in the time of Alexander the Great.

Government

Because Greek city-states were often separated from each other by mountain ranges,

► The map shows the extent of Greek civilization around the Aegean Sea. Colonies typically consisted of cities surrounded by farmland, which were under the control of settlers. These colonies were linked to the Greek mainland city where the settlers originally came from.

they developed in different ways, even though they shared the same language and worshiped the same gods.

Some city-states were ruled by a king and thus were monarchies. The word *monarchy* comes from two Greek words meaning "rule" and "alone." Other city-states were ruled by rich, landowning families, a type of government called aristocracy (*aristos* means "best"). Rule by someone who seizes power for himself is known as tyranny. If a small group seizes power, the government is an oligarchy (*oligos* means "few").

Athens passed through some of these forms of government before finally developing democracy, a type of government in which every citizen had a say in what the laws should be (*demos* is the Greek for "people").

▼ *The Pnyx in Athens, meeting place for the Ecclesia, or Assembly. Here up to six thousand Athenian citizens met about four times a month to discuss and vote on the laws that were to govern them.*

CLASSICAL GREECE

c. 1200 BCE
Troy is destroyed by the Greeks.

776 BCE
First Olympic Games.

c. 700 BCE
Homer composes the *Iliad* and the *Odyssey*.

490 BCE
Battle of Marathon: Athenians defeat Persian invasion of Greece.

480 BCE
Battle of Thermopylae: Greeks are defeated, Athens is destroyed.

480 BCE
Sea battle of Salamis: Persians are defeated.

479 BCE
Battle of Plataea: final defeat of Persians.

c. 478–430 BCE
Athens is at the peak of her power, ruled as a democracy.

431–404 BCE
Peloponnesian War between Athens and Sparta: Sparta is triumphant.

371 BCE
Battle of Leuktra: Sparta is defeated by Thebes.

338 BCE
Philip of Macedon defeats combined Greek army at Battle of Chaeronea.

336 BCE
Alexander the Great becomes king of Macedonia and begins conquest of Persia.

XENOPHON
c. 428–c. 354 BCE

Xenophon was born into an aristocratic Athenian family. He became a pupil of the philosopher Socrates and a member of the Athenian cavalry. However, he left Athens and served first the Persians and then the Spartans against Athens. He was exiled by the Athenians, yet as relations between Athens and Sparta improved, he may have been allowed to return to Athens, where he died.

He is famous for the books he wrote during his extraordinary life: seven on the history of Greece and others on a variety of subjects, including hare hunting, horsemanship, and an imaginary account of a drinking party with Socrates called *The Symposium*.

Although Athenian democracy did not include voting rights for women or slaves, it was the most advanced form of government in Greece and has been a model for democratic countries ever since.

Religion

The ancient Greeks believed in many different gods, each controlling a different area of life. Of these there were twelve who were regarded as the most important. They were called Olympians because it was believed they lived on the top of Mount Olympus. The Olympians were led by Zeus and his wife, Hera. Each of the major gods was worshiped at temples dedicated to them.

Below the Olympians were many thousands of lesser gods, as each stream, field, and tree had its own spirit. During the classical period some philosophers began to question the existence of the gods as the Greeks understood them and even whether there were gods at all.

Science, Medicine, and Philosophy

The Greeks made some very important scientific discoveries. In the classical period Anaxagoras (500–428 BCE) worked out that the sun was made of fire and that the moon reflected the sun's light. Hippocrates (c. 460–377 BCE) realized that illness was due not to the anger of the gods but to the faulty working of the body. He considered nature the best healer, so proper food and exercise were important to him. The Hippocratic oath, which embodies a code of conduct of a doctor toward a patient, was taken by Western doctors until well into the twentieth century.

Socrates (470–399 BCE) is one of the best-known philosophers from this period. After Socrates' death, his ideas were written down by his disciple Plato (427–347 BCE). Plato set up a school called the Academy. He believed, among many other things, that the best form of government was not democracy but rule by the wise.

▶ A fourth-century-BCE relief showing a doctor tending to the damaged arm of a patient. Another patient lies on a couch attended by a nurse. Sculptures like these were brought by the sick to healing sites as an offering to the gods in hope of or in thanks for a cure.

GYMNASIA

The gymnasium was a public exercise and meeting area, often located near an athletic stadium or sports ground, with a running track, jumping pits, and a range for discus and javelin throwing. There might also be a wrestling area called a palaestra. Gymnasia had changing rooms, bathrooms, and a dust room for dusting over the olive oil the athletes applied to their bodies before exercise. There was a room for ball games and another with punchballs for boxing. Gymnasia were popular places for men to meet and talk, as many had colonnades to provide shelter from the sun. The philosopher Plato set up his Academy at one of the three Athenian gymnasia.

Men and Women

In Athens all adult male citizens could expect to play some part in the running of the city for at least a year of their lives. In their free time men often exercised at the gymnasium. Here, in Athens especially, the men could also listen to the ideas of teachers and philosophers. Alternatively, they could spend time at the agora, the town center and marketplace, another popular meeting point. There were also all-male drinking parties, called symposia, held in private homes.

Women had little or no legal and political power in ancient Greece. They were always under the control of a male relative, who may have been their father, husband, brother, or even their son, depending on the woman's age and situation. Women could not take part in the running of their city. Most of a family's property was controlled by men.

A wife's duty was to oversee the running of the household. In a rich home her duties might include supervising many slaves, as well as spinning and weaving. She might leave the house only occasionally and then accompanied by a slave.

▼ *This fifth-century-BCE vase painting shows a young woman checking her appearance in a mirror while holding a jewelry or makeup box. Domestic scenes like this were a favorite subject for vase painters.*

▲ On this small fifth-century-BCE vase, two boys are taking a rest from their play carts and sharing some grapes.

Homer. They were also taught arithmetic, which was a difficult subject because the Greeks used letters for numbers and had no zero. An abacus was used for harder calculations.

Music and dancing were very important and so was physical training at the gymnasium. Teachers were present at the gymnasium to teach any who were interested, and here a boy could receive his higher education. At eighteen an Athenian boy would join the army for a few years.

Spartan schooling was quite different from Athenian. The Spartans placed the highest importance on developing physical strength and endurance. Boys were placed in barracks from the age of seven and did not leave the army until they were thirty. Spartan girls were taught to run, wrestle, and throw the javelin. The Spartans believed fit girls would give birth to strong children later on.

Homes

Greek houses were usually built from mud bricks. Larger houses were built around a central courtyard, which might have an altar for household prayers. Richer homes often had two stories, with separate living rooms for men and women. Outside the front door there was usually a small statue of the god Hermes to protect the house from evil.

The finest room in the house was the *andron*, where the men would entertain their guests. The floor might be a mosaic, and the walls were often decorated with tapestries woven by the women of the house. The women's living room, the *gynaeceum*, was used for spinning and weaving, as well as entertaining friends.

Furniture included chairs, stools, low tables, and couches for reclining. Rooms

Poorer women led a very different life. They fetched their own water from the well and did their own shopping and thus met far more people than rich women.

Children

Boys from wealthy families started school at about six. Girls were taught at home by their mother. The pupils sat on stools without a desk and scratched their lessons on a wax tablet with a stylus. They were taught to read and write and memorized large amounts of poetry, especially by were lit by oil lamps and heated by portable stoves. Some homes had a bathroom containing a terra-cotta bath.

Food and Farming

Greece is a mountainous country with long, hot, dry summers. Because of this combination of land and climate, large areas are unsuitable for agriculture, and farming is largely kept to the valley bottoms and the fertile inland and coastal plains.

As in all societies in the ancient world, most Greeks made their living from family-owned farms. These were usually small, supporting just the family, and worked by the family with a little help from hired workers or slaves.

ATTITUDES TOWARD CHILDREN ARE REVEALED IN THIS EXTRACT FROM THE WRITINGS OF THE PHILOSOPHER PLATO:

Right from the time you are old enough to understand what they say to you, your nurse, your mother, your tutor, and your father all try to make you as good as possible. Whatever you do or say, they are always there to put you right by saying: "This is right; that is wrong. This is the decent thing to do; that is shocking. This is polite; that is rude. Do this; don't do that." As long as you do what you are told, there is no trouble. But if you don't, they threaten you and beat you into shape, as if you were a twisted wooden plank.

PLATO, PROTAGORAS

▼ A sixth-century-BCE terra-cotta model of a plow being pulled by two oxen while the plowman steers. This method of plowing was used throughout the ancient world.

Although Greeks reared cattle, most important were their crops: grapes, olives, and grain, usually barley for bread. Olives were grown to make olive oil for use in cooking and in oil lamps. Grapes were grown for wine, the most common drink.

Art and Drama

The artistic center of classical Greece was Athens. Here many of the most famous artists, writers, painters, potters, architects, and sculptors could be found. Greek wall paintings have all perished over time, but the painted pots were fired in an oven and so were preserved. Athenian clay was rich in iron, which turns red on firing. A thin coat of this clay used as paint, called slip, would turn black when painted over the pots and fired; these pots are called either red or black figure. All sorts of scenes were painted on these pots. They give a vivid picture of life at that time.

Athenian playwrights such as Aeschylus (525–455 BCE), Sophocles (496–405 BCE), Euripides (485–406 BCE), and Aristophanes (c. 450–386 BCE) were celebrated in their own time and have remained famous ever since. They wrote their tragic, funny, and sometimes satirical plays for competitions held in huge open-air theaters. Their plays are performed to this day.

◀ These two clay figures depict comedy actors. The masks they wear were often made from strips of linen fixed with glue and first built up on the actor's head. In some plays the masks were made from silver or gold in order to impress the audience.

Clothes and Jewelry

Greek women wore chitons, which were rectangular pieces of woven wool or linen with a hole cut in the center for the head. Very rich women wore cotton or silk imported from the East. Belts, brooches, and buttons were used to gather the material in a variety of attractive ways. Men often wore a simple knee-length tunic with a belt. Both men and women often wore a himation, a type of cloak. It might be light and short or heavy and long with a hood for protection against the cold.

Greek jewelry has been found in tombs, buried with its owners. For the rich, jewelry was made from precious metals or ivory. Poorer people wore jewelry made from cheaper metals or bone.

Slavery

Slaves probably formed about a quarter of the population of ancient Greece. A person became a slave in a variety of ways. A slave may have been captured in battle or on

▲ A beautifully crafted fourth-century-BCE Greek necklace of golden droplets with a bull's head medallion in the center.

deliberate slave raids. A person might be born into slavery as the child of a slave, or a freeman might be sold into slavery to pay his debts (although this practice was made illegal in Athens).

The quality of slaves' lives greatly depended on the attitudes of their owners and the type of jobs they did. A new slave might be greeted at his or her new home with small gifts and might be paid a small wage that could be saved to buy freedom. Slaves who worked on the Parthenon and other famous buildings in Athens were paid as much as the freemen working alongside them, although most of this money went to the slaves' owners. Some slaves were treated harshly, particularly those who worked in mines or quarries, and some might literally be worked to death.

A RECORD, FROM AN ANCIENT GREEK INSCRIPTION, OF A LIST OF SLAVES SOLD TO PAY A NOBLEMAN'S DEBTS IN 414 BCE:

Nationality	Value
Thracian female	165 dr
Thracian male	170 dr
Syrian male	240 dr
Carian male	105 dr
Illyrian male	161 dr
Carian male (young)	174 dr
Carian infant	72 dr

(IN 414 BCE ONE DRACHMA ["DR"] WAS A DAY'S PAY FOR A SKILLED CRAFTSMAN, AND TEN DRACHMAS MIGHT BUY A WOOLEN CLOAK.)

SEE ALSO

• Agamemnon • Aristotle • Athens • Delphi • Greek Mythology
• Greek Philosophy • Iliad and Odyssey • Olympia • Pericles
• Plato • Socrates • Sparta • Troy • Zeus

Greek Mythology

Greek myths began as spoken stories that were passed on from generation to generation. They were eventually written down by poets, such as Homer, and playwrights, such as Sophocles. Later, Roman poets, especially Ovid and Virgil, wrote their own versions of the Greek myths. Many scenes from these myths have survived in Greek art.

Myths of the Creation

There are several Greek creation myths. According to one the universe began with the goddess Night, in the form of a huge black-winged bird. Moved by the Wind, she laid a silver egg from which hatched Eros, god of love. Eros then revealed the world, previously hidden in the egg. Above was Chaos (Greek for "it yawns"), or Emptiness. Below was the earth.

Out of Chaos came Gaia, Mother Earth. She gave birth to the sky god Ouranos, who became her husband. They had children, the Titans, but Ouranos hated them and stuffed them back into the earth. So Gaia armed the youngest, Cronus, with a sickle, with which he overthrew his father and freed his brothers and sisters.

Cronus, however, was as bad as his father. Fearing a prophecy that he would be overthrown by one of his children, he swallowed them all. Fortunately, his wife, Rhea, tricked him by giving him a stone wrapped in cloth instead of the youngest son, Zeus. She hid Zeus in a cave. When he grew up, he forced Cronus to release the swallowed children. Zeus became the king of this new generation of gods, the Olympians.

▶ A second-century-BCE frieze showing the Olympian goddess Athena in the battle between the new Olympian gods and the older generation — the Titans. Here she separates Alcyoneus from Gaia (Mother Earth) so that he cannot be immortal.

ATHENA

THE OLYMPIAN GODS

Zeus and twelve other gods lived on Mount Olympus:

ZEUS *God of thunder and ruler of the gods*

POSEIDON *God of the sea and of earthquakes*

HEPHAESTUS *God of fire and metalwork*

HERMES *Messenger of the gods*

ARES *God of war*

APOLLO *God of light, truth, and healing*

DIONYSUS *God of wine and fertility*

HERA *Wife of Zeus and queen of the gods*

ATHENA *Goddess of wisdom and war*

ARTEMIS *Goddess of the moon and of hunting*

DEMETER *Goddess of agriculture*

APHRODITE *Goddess of love*

HESTIA *Goddess of the hearth*

▼ A fourth-century-BCE marble head of the god Apollo. As god of truth, Apollo was also associated with prophecy. People traveled from all over Greece to consult Apollo's oracle in his shrine at Delphi.

Myths of the Olympian Gods

The Olympian gods were far from perfect. They were affected by jealousy, anger, and desire and often used manipulation and trickery to get what they wanted. Even Zeus was not above this behavior. Although married to Hera, he often pursued beautiful nymphs and mortal women. Hera took her revenge by punishing the children that Zeus fathered by these women.

Of all the gods Hermes was the most accomplished trickster. As a baby he stole Apollo's cattle and hid them in a cave. To fool pursuers he tied brushwood onto his feet to disguise his footprints and made the cattle walk backwards. Apollo eventually forgave him when Hermes gave him a lyre made from a tortoise shell.

In another story of discord, Hades, lord of the underworld, enticed the beautiful young goddess Persephone with a wonderful narcissus flower. When she reached for it, he burst out of the ground in his chariot and carried her off. Her mother, Demeter, was grief stricken. Eventually it was agreed that Persephone would spend half of each year in the underworld.

Gods and Mortals

Gods often took human women for their lovers. Less often, goddesses fell in love with men. However, the beauty of a goddess was usually too much for men to cope with. Seeing a goddess in her full splendor was the ruin of the huntsman Actaeon. He came upon Artemis bathing with her maidens in the forest. She was furious and turned him into a stag. His own hounds then tore him to pieces.

A rare happy ending to a love between a god and a mortal occurred for Eros and his human lover, Psyche. Eros's mother, Aphrodite, was jealous and set Psyche seemingly impossible tasks. One was to sort a roomful of mixed seeds into separate piles. In this task Psyche was helped by ants. In the end she passed all the tests, and Zeus made her immortal so that Aphrodite would no longer consider her an unworthy daughter-in-law.

Hero Myths

Many Greek hero myths probably began as factual stories. As they were retold, they began to involve the gods, and soon the stories merged. In the typical hero myth, the hero is at first poor and has either lost touch with his real parents or is an orphan. Often he goes to meet his father or a father figure and is sent on a dangerous mission. He may be helped or hindered by the gods.

Theseus grew up not knowing his father, King Aegeus of Athens. However, Aegeus had hidden a sword and sandals under a rock for his son to find if he grew strong enough to lift it. Facing many dangers along the way, Theseus traveled to Athens and found his father. He then went to Crete as part of a group of young men and women intended to be fed to a monster, the Minotaur. When he arrived, the king's daughter, Ariadne, gave him a ball of thread. Unwinding the thread, he entered the labyrinth, an underground maze in which the Minotaur lived. He killed the Minotaur and then found his way out by following the thread.

Another hero separated from his parents and sent on a quest was Jason, who was told to fetch the Golden Fleece, the skin of a magical talking sheep. He collected a shipload of heroes, the Argonauts, including Heracles (also known as Hercules). They faced many dangers before finding the fleece with the help of the goddess Hera and the sorceress Medea.

THE HERO PERSEUS WAS A SON OF ZEUS. HIS MOTHER'S FATHER SET MOTHER AND SON ADRIFT ON THE OCEAN. WHEN PERSEUS GREW UP, HE WAS SENT TO FETCH THE HEAD OF THE SNAKE-HAIRED GORGON, MEDUSA. HE SUCCEEDED WITH HELP FROM ATHENA AND HERMES. FLYING HOME BY MEANS OF HERMES'S WINGED SANDALS, HE FELL IN LOVE WITH THE BEAUTIFUL ANDROMEDA AND SAVED HER FROM A SEA MONSTER:

Condemned to suffer for her mother's boast,
Andromeda was fastened to a rock.
When Perseus saw her, had a little breeze
Not stirred her hair, her eyes not overflowed
With quivering tears, he would have thought she was
A marble statue. Before he knew it, love
Sprang up. He gazed enchanted. Overcome
By beauty so unusual and rare, he
Almost forgot to hover in the air.

OVID, METAMORPHOSES

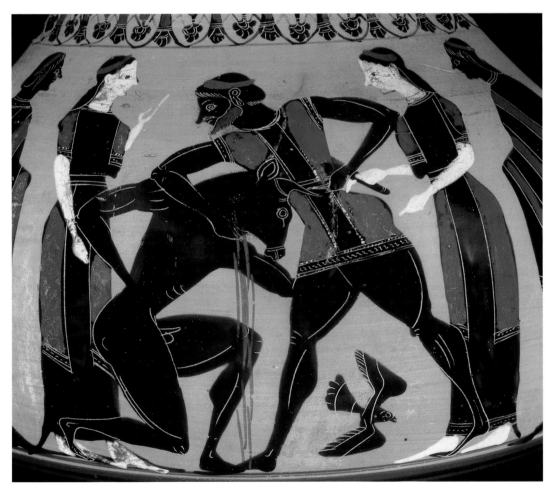

◀ A vase painting from 540–530 BCE showing the hero Theseus stabbing the Minotaur.

SEE ALSO
• Agamemnon
• Athena
• Greece, Classical
• Iliad and Odyssey
• Mythology
• Odysseus • Troy
• Zeus

Greek Philosophy

The word *philosophy* comes from the Greek words *philia*, "love," and *sophia*, "wisdom." In ancient Greece a philosopher was originally anyone who engaged in mental activity; philosophers included thinkers and those involved in the arts and sciences. Later on, *philosophy* came to mean a search for the truth without reference to divine or religious considerations, much as it still does.

▼ *A later engraving of a bust of the early Greek philosopher Thales (c. 640–546 BCE). In the opinion of Aristotle, Thales was the father of Greek philosophy.*

Early Greek Philosophers

The first Greek philosophers were scientists. One of these was Thales (c. 640–546 BCE), who asked himself what the earth was made of. He concluded it was made of water, because when one digs, one always reaches water. Anaximenes, who lived around 540 BCE, believed the earth was made of air; he claimed that stones were simply air in its most solid form. Democritus (c. 460–370 BCE) said the earth was made of atoms – indestructible, indivisible particles – and the spaces between them.

For Democritus and other thinkers, religious or traditional explanations could no longer be taken for granted. They believed events were not caused by the gods but occurred for reasons to be found in nature. A rainbow, according to these thinkers, was not the goddess Juno but a multicolored cloud. According to Anaxagoras (c. 500–428 BCE) the sun was not Helios pulling a chariot; it was a red-hot stone.

The philosophers were not always correct in their explanations for natural events, but they were the first to try to explain them without referring to religion. Thales believed that a magnet had a soul because it could move things. Xenophanes said that, just as new clouds rise and pass by, the sun that rose and passed overhead was a new one each day.

Socrates

The three great figures of Greek philosophy were Socrates, Plato, and Aristotle. The first of these, Socrates, lived from around 470 to

399 BCE. He did not write anything down, and most of what is known about Socrates comes from his friend and pupil Plato (c. 429–347 BCE), who wrote down his conversations, or dialogues, with Socrates.

These dialogues record the philosophical discussions between Socrates and his friends. Socrates' questions, unlike those of earlier philosophers, were not about the workings of nature, the sun, or the stars but about human concerns. He asked, for example, what is the best kind of government? What is courage? Can one teach people to be better?

Rather than offering an opinion, Socrates led the discussion by asking his friends questions. He insisted that before discussing any question, it was necessary to ask another: 'How can you be sure you know anything at all?' Socrates challenged people by asking them to define the words they used. His method exposed inconsistencies in people's beliefs, especially in how they used words like *right* and *wrong*.

Plato

Plato's early dialogues presented Socrates' ideas in written form. In Plato's later works, the character of Socrates expresses Plato's own views. In *The Republic* Plato explores the meaning of justice and its role in the creation of an ideal state. Plato, in the voice of Socrates, suggests that justice on earth is only a poor copy of real, eternal justice. In other works Plato teaches that the objects and ideas of this world are imperfect copies of their equivalent forms in the spirit world, which are timeless and unchanging.

▶ An Italian painting from about 1780 CE, in which the painter imagines Socrates reprimanding – perhaps for his unruly ways – his young friend the famous general Alcibiades, whose life Socrates once saved in battle.

XENOPHANES WAS A WANDERING POET OF THE MID-SIXTH CENTURY BCE WHO WROTE MANY VERSES THAT OTHERS, THEN AND SINCE, HAVE CONSIDERED TO BE PHILOSOPHY:

Human beings think of gods as being like themselves,
with clothes and language
and a bodily shape like their own,
but if cows or horses or lions had hands
and could draw with their hands
and create the kind of representations humans make,
then horses making drawing of their gods
would draw them like horses,
and cows would draw their gods in the form of cows.

Aristotle

The third great philosopher of this period, Aristotle (c. 384–322), was a pupil of Plato and a man with knowledge of a great many subjects. Aristotle believed that philosophy was about the discovery of knowledge through the application of logic. He invented a system of logic and was the first thinker to clearly separate philosophy from science. Unlike Plato, he believed that truth was not to be found in the spirit world but could be discovered by the study of nature. He insisted that any science should collect and classify, even the science of politics. He said, "From collections of constitutions we examine what sort of thing preserves and what destroys cities."

Hellenistic Philosophy

In the Hellenistic age, which lasted from around 300 to 150 BCE, Greek philosophers became more interested in the relationship between the individual and society, and they recommended different ways of living. The Stoics were a group who believed that evils such as pain and poverty were not to be feared or avoided but accepted with *apatheia*, that is, "absence of passion." The Stoics were also ahead of their time in believing in the equality of all humanity.

Another group, the Epicureans, believed in living simply and privately, quietly pursuing pleasure and avoiding politics or anything that brought frustration or anxiety. They did not believe in the immortality of the soul or in an afterlife.

◀ *A marble copy by the Roman sculptor Chrysippus of a third-century-BCE bust of the philosopher Epicurus, who taught that the main aim of life was to attain peace of mind.*

GREEK PHILOSOPHY AND WRITING

Greek philosophy came into existence in many different ways. Little of it was written in the form of a book with an author, as current works of philosophy are. Although much Greek philosophy was written down, a large amount of it was not. No writing of Thales survives, nor does any original work by Democritus.

Of the philosophy that was written down, not all of it was expressed in prose. Xenophanes, Empedocles (c. 493–c. 433), and Parmenides (sixth century BCE) expressed their ideas in poetry. Plato wrote dialogues, expressing his ideas through dramatized conversations. Aristotle's works were written in prose but mostly in the form of lecture notes, reorganized into books by later scholars.

Socrates lacked faith in the written word, probably because writing was a fairly new means of communication in his day. There was uncertainty and suspicion about how it might affect thinking. Socrates noted that in conversation ideas can be challenged. On the other hand, the writer's ideas cannot, because the writer is absent.

Legacy

The creative era of Greek philosophy had come to an end in 529 CE, when the Roman emperor Justinian banned the teaching of all "pagan," that is, non-Christian, philosophy. However, the influence of Greek philosophy became increasingly widespread. Greek philosophy was studied in Islamic countries and in medieval Europe, and it is studied still.

◀ An eighteenth-century painting depicting Alexander the Great meeting the Cynic philospher Diogenes (c. 400–325 BCE), who allegedly lived in a tub or jar. Alexander promises Diogenes whatever he requests. Diogenes asks Alexander to move to one side — he is blocking out the sun.

SEE ALSO

- Aristotle • Greece, Classical • Plato
- Roman Philosophy • Science • Socrates

Gupta Empire

Five hundred years after the fall of India's first empire, the Mauryan Empire, a second Indian empire was established by a family of kings called the Guptas. For almost two hundred years, from 320 to 550 CE, the Guptas provided stable rule for a large area of India. This period was a time of great achievements in art, science, and literature. Gupta kings boasted in their inscriptions that "perfection has been reached," and many people still think of the Gupta period as India's golden age.

Conquests

The Gupta Empire was created by the second Gupta ruler, Samudra Gupta, who reigned from around 335 until about 380 CE and spent more than forty years on military campaigns conquering one kingdom after another.

Samudra Gupta and the kings who followed him ruled their empire as overlords. Conquered kings were allowed to continue ruling their own territories but were expected to pay tribute to the Gupta kings. This tribute was used to pay for further wars of conquest. Lesser kings were also required to pay their respects by visiting the Guptas in the audience halls of their palaces and bowing before them. One of the later kings, Skanda Gupta, who ruled from about 455 to 467, boasted that his audience hall was "shaken by the wind caused by the falling down [in bowing] of the heads of a hundred kings."

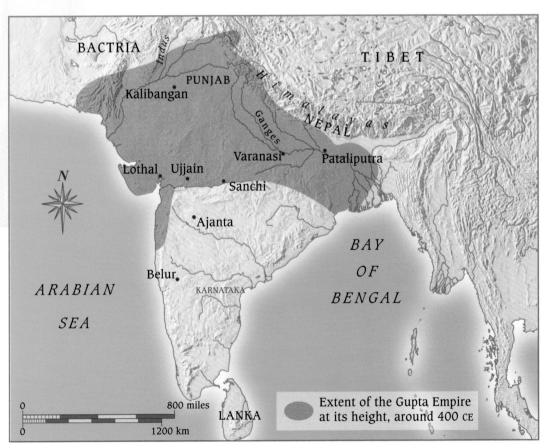

▶ The Gupta Empire at its height.

CHANDRA GUPTA I
REIGNED 320–335 CE

Confusingly, the founder of the Gupta Empire was named Chandragupta, as was the founder of the earlier Mauryan Empire. Chandragupta may have taken this name deliberately, for the Guptas knew about and admired the Mauryans. To distinguish between the two rulers, the Gupta emperor's name is usually written as two words, Chandra Gupta.

Around 320 CE Chandra Gupta inherited a small kingdom on the banks of the Ganges in northeastern India. By marrying a princess named Kumuradevi, who was heir to the neighboring kingdom, he was able to double the size of his territory. He ruled the whole Ganges valley from the ancient city of Pataliputra, which became the Gupta capital. It was in Pataliputra that Chandra Gupta assumed the new title Maharajadhirajah, which means "great king of kings."

GUPTA EMPIRE

320–335 CE
Reign of Chandra Gupta I.

335–c. 380 CE
Reign of Samudra Gupta, who conquers much of northern and eastern India.

c. 380 CE
Short reign of Rama Gupta.

c. 380–c. 415 CE
Reign of Chandra Gupta II, whose conquests extend the empire yet further.

◀ *Samudra Gupta was the first emperor to mint gold coins. This one shows a horse; the earliest Guptas sacrificed horses to the Hindu gods.*

c. 415–c. 455 CE
Reign of Kumara Gupta. India is attacked by the White Huns. Kumara Gupta dies in the middle of the war.

c. 455–c. 467 CE
Reign of Skanda Gupta, who drives out the White Huns.

c. 467–c. 475 CE
Struggles for the throne.

c. 475–c. 495 CE
Reign of Budha Gupta.

c. 495–550 CE
The empire breaks up as the White Huns conquer northern India and local kings no longer accept Gupta overlordship.

Science and the Arts

Gupta mathematicians were the most advanced in the world. Their invention of the concept of zero made arithmetic much simpler. The late Gupta period was the time of the great Indian astronomer and mathematician Aryabhata (476–550 CE). He correctly reasoned that the apparent movement of the stars was caused by the earth spinning on its axis and that the moon and the planets shone by the reflected light of the sun. Aryabhata also calculated the length of the solar year as 365.358 days, the most accurate measurement made to that time.

▼ *A fifth-century statue of a Hindu goddess, perhaps Paravati, wife of Shiva. Although the Guptas allowed freedom of worship, they promoted Hinduism. As a result, Buddhism began to die out as an Indian religion.*

Literature also flourished at the Gupta court, where the most famous ancient Indian poet, Kalidasa (c. 400 CE), wrote his plays and poems. In art skilled sculptors made beautiful seated statues of the Buddha and the first statues of the Hindu gods.

Society

Under the Guptas, India was a well-ruled and peaceful society. Crafts and trade were controlled by guilds, which were societies that set prices, made sure that craftspeople were properly trained, and checked that goods on sale were of an acceptable quality. The Gupta kings used their wealth to benefit the people; they built resting places on the roads for travelers and hospitals that provided free health care.

Decline

In the 450s CE the Guptas were attacked by the White Huns, a warlike people from central Asia. The invaders were driven out by Skanda Gupta, but the victory was temporary. Shortly before 500 CE the White Huns returned, overrunning northern India and sacking Pataliputra. The empire fell apart, as local kings no longer accepted Gupta overlordship. India was once more split up into many small kingdoms that were often at war with each other. The golden age was over.

Hadrian

Rome had few emperors as capable as Hadrian, who reigned from 117 to 138 CE. He was an intelligent and strong leader, and his reign was one of the great periods in the history of the Roman Empire.

Hadrian's Rise to Power

Hadrian was born in 76 CE, probably in Rome. His father died when he was ten, after which two guardians brought him up. One was Trajan, his father's cousin, who some years later became emperor (reigned 98–117). This connection was to prove valuable in Hadrian's own rise to power, since Trajan came to regard Hadrian as his son.

Hadrian was well educated. He was so interested in anything to do with Greece that he earned the nickname Greekling. As a young man he served with distinction in the Roman army, and Emperor Trajan appointed him governor of the province of Syria.

Trajan died in 117 CE. Before an emperor died, he was supposed to name his successor, but it is not certain whether Trajan ever did. However, the day after Trajan's death, it was announced that Hadrian was to be the new emperor. Hadrian's reign began badly when four senators were executed in Rome for allegedly plotting his overthrow. Hadrian denied any involvement in their death, but many senators did not believe him.

The Traveling Emperor

The Roman Empire reached its greatest extent during the reign of Trajan. However, the larger it grew, the harder and more costly it was to control. Instead of enlarging the empire, Hadrian's policy was to establish boundaries for it. Some of these were natural, such as rivers; others, like

Hadrian's Wall in northern Britain, were man-made. He secured the empire along its frontiers, and through this policy the Roman world entered a time of peace and stability.

◄ Hadrian was the first Roman emperor shown with a beard; those before him were clean shaven. He may have grown a beard because Greek men wore beards and he liked anything and everything to do with Greece.

Hadrian was hardly ever in Rome or even Italy. He spent more than half his reign traveling, visiting almost every province in the empire. By so doing he gained firsthand knowledge of the different peoples of the Roman world and the lands within it.

SEE ALSO
- Hadrian's Wall
- Roman Republic and Empire

▲ At Tibur (present-day Tivoli), fifteen miles (24 km) east of Rome, Hadrian built a massive villa, containing around one hundred separate buildings. Guests looked out over this ornamental pool from their rooms.

Hadrian's Final Years

In 134 CE, after one of his rare visits to Rome, Hadrian set out for the eastern province of Judaea, where he ended an uprising led by the Jewish leader Shimon Bar Kokhba (died 135). It was almost the only war of his reign.

Hadrian returned to Rome in 136, aged sixty and in ill health. After his death in 138, the Roman Senate tried to destroy his reputation. Rome's senators had not forgotten the deaths of their four colleagues at the start of Hadrian's reign, and they wanted revenge against the man they held responsible. However, Hadrian's successor, Antoninus Pius (reigned 138–161) prevented any plot from succeeding, and Hadrian passed into history as one of Rome's "good" emperors.

THE FOLLOWING IS A DESCRIPTION OF HADRIAN WRITTEN BY AN ANONYMOUS AUTHOR IN THE FOURTH CENTURY CE:

He was tall of stature and elegant in appearance; his hair was curled on a comb, and he wore a full beard to cover up the natural blemishes on his face; and he was very strongly built. He rode and walked a great deal and always kept himself in training by the use of arms and the javelin. He also hunted, and he used often to kill a lion with his own hand, but once in a hunt he broke his collarbone and a rib; these hunts of his he always shared with his friends.

HISTORIA AUGUSTA

Hadrian's Wall

The northern frontier of the Roman Empire was marked by a wall in Britain. Built during the reign of Emperor Hadrian (117–138 CE), the wall separated the northern barbarians from the Romans for nearly three hundred years.

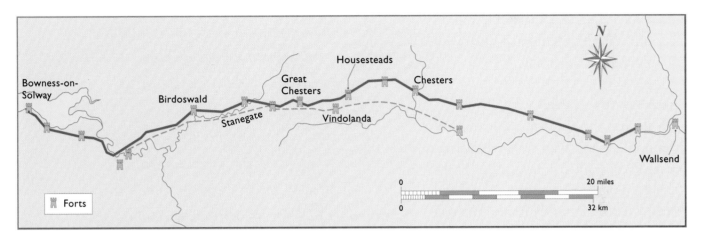

Britain in the Roman Empire

The Roman conquest of Britain began in 43 CE. By the 80s CE much of the island was under Roman control, the British tribes proving no match in open battle against the highly organized and well-armed Roman army. Britain was mostly pacified, but thanks to an uprising in the province of Dacia (present-day Romania and Hungary), troops were withdrawn to fight a war there. Around 100 the Roman army withdrew from Scotland to a frontier line established twenty years earlier between the Tyne River on the east coast and the Solway Firth on the west coast. This old frontier was a military road known later as the Stanegate, a name that means "stone way," along which forts had been built.

Edge of Empire

When Hadrian came to power, there was already unrest in northern Britain. Roman forces defeated the rebels, but the threat of trouble remained. In 122 Hadrian came to Britain as part of a long-term tour of the provinces of the Roman Empire. Unlike emperors before him, Hadrian had no intention of continuing to enlarge Rome's overseas territories. Instead he adopted a policy of protecting the Roman world by establishing frontiers at its limits. In Britain, Hadrian ordered a wall to be built to mark Rome's northern frontier. Its purpose was political, not military. It represented the edge of empire, a fixed line that separated uncivilized barbarians to the north from the civilized people of the Roman world.

Building the Wall

Hadrian's Wall runs for seventy-three miles (117 km) from modern-day Wallsend to Bowness-on-Solway. It was built slightly north of the Stanegate military road, on higher ground. Legionaries stationed in Britain began building the wall in 122, and it took over ten years to complete. In its final state it was a stone wall with a thickness of eight to ten feet (2.4–3 m) and a height of fourteen to fifteen feet

▲ The route of Hadrian's Wall, showing the course of the Stanegate military road and the positions of the forts.

(4.25–4.65 m). Milecastles, which were fortified gateways housing from eight to thirty-two men, were built at every Roman mile, or 1,620 yards (1,480 m), and a pair of lookout towers lay between them. Seventeen forts lay along the wall, each housing five hundred to a thousand troops. A deep ditch was dug to the north, while to the south was a flat-bottomed ditch with earth mounds on either side.

The Abandoned Wall

Even during the Roman occupation of Britain, Hadrian's Wall suffered neglect, and repairs were often necessary. By 411 the Roman Empire was close to collapse, and Britain was abandoned by Rome. The wall no longer had a purpose, and for the next fifteen hundred years its stones were carted away to provide building materials in nearby towns and villages.

▼ *Hadrian's Wall was one of several fixed boundaries, or* limes, *built at the edges of the Roman Empire.*

THE VINDOLANDA WRITING TABLETS

Vindolanda was one of the seventeen large forts near Hadrian's Wall. Buried in the fort's waterlogged soil archaeologists have discovered almost two thousand wooden writing tablets — more than have been found anywhere else in the Roman Empire. Preserved on them are traces of handwriting that give a real picture of life for soldiers and civilians on the Roman Empire's northern frontier. While one man grumbles about the lack of beer, another is sent woolen socks and underpants. As for the British, a Roman writer calls them "wretched Britons."

SEE ALSO
- Boudicca • Hadrian
- Roman Republic and Empire

Hannibal

Hannibal (247–c. 182 BCE) was a military leader whose army crossed the Mediterranean Sea and the Alps to fight the Romans in Italy. Many historians consider him one of the greatest generals in history.

The Punic Wars

In the third and second centuries BCE, Carthage, a Phoenician city in North Africa (in modern-day Tunisia), fought with Rome over control of the Mediterranean region. Their conflicts are known as the Punic Wars. The First Punic War (264–241 BCE) ended in defeat for the Carthaginians, who lost control of the island of Sicily. To compensate for this loss, Hamilcar Barca (c. 270–c. 229 BCE), the Carthaginian general, established colonies in Spain, from where an attack could be mounted on Rome.

Hannibal's Early Life

Hannibal was the eldest son of Hamilcar Barca. In 237 BCE the nine-year-old boy was with his father and the Carthaginian army in Spain, where he is said to have sworn an oath of hostility against Rome. Hamilcar Barca drowned in about 229 BCE. Command of the army then passed to Hasdrubal (Hamilcar Barca's son-in-law) and, after his murder in 221 BCE, to the twenty-five-year-old Hannibal.

Hannibal's War

In 219 BCE Hannibal attacked Saguntum in eastern Spain. The town was loyal to Rome, and the Romans saw the attack as an act of war. It sparked off the Second Punic War (218–201 BCE). In June 218 BCE Hannibal led his forces toward Italy, intent on defeating the Romans on their own territory. That October he crossed the Alps at the head of between 35,000 and 40,000 infantry, about 8,000 cavalry, and 37 war elephants, only one of which, named Surus, survived the hazardous crossing.

▼ Hannibal's failure was due, in part, to lack of support from his allies and to Carthage's failure to send reinforcements.

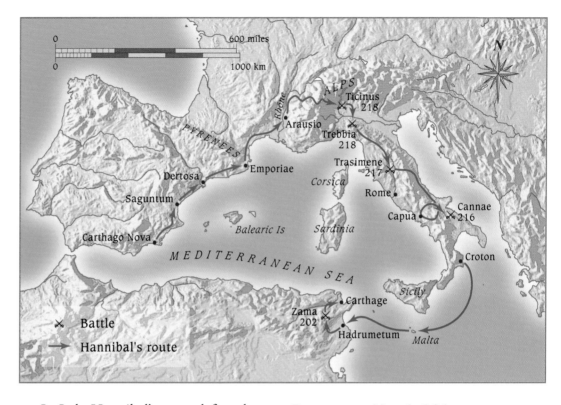

▶ *The route taken by Hannibal, including the sites of his famous battles.*

SEE ALSO
- Carthage
- Phoenicians
- Roman Republic and Empire

In Italy Hannibal's army defeated one Roman force after another, in battles at Ticinus (218 BCE), Trebia (218), and Trasimene (217). At the Battle of Cannae (216) he almost wiped out the entire Roman army, killing around fifty thousand soldiers and taking perhaps twenty thousand prisoner. Following this victory, Hannibal camped within three miles of Rome and even rode up to the city walls with his cavalry. Many Romans believed their city was about to be sacked.

THE FOLLOWING IS PART OF A DESCRIPTION OF HANNIBAL'S CROSSING OF THE ALPS, WRITTEN BY THE ROMAN HISTORIAN, LIVY (59 BCE–17 CE):

The elephants were both a blessing and a curse, for though getting them along the narrow tracks caused delay, they protected the troops as the natives, who had not seen such creatures before, were afraid to come near them. After nine days' climb Hannibal's army reached the snow-covered summit of the pass.

LIVY, *HISTORY OF ROME FROM ITS FOUNDATION*, BOOK 21

Retreat to North Africa

After losing at Cannae, Roman tactics changed. Instead of fighting the invader, the Roman army forced Hannibal into futile chases around the country, a ploy that exhausted his troops and his supplies. He spent four years in the south of Italy, effectively cornered. In 204 BCE the Roman general Scipio Africanus (236–183 BCE) led an army of thirty thousand Romans against Carthage. This move by the Romans took the war directly to the Carthaginians. Hannibal, recalled home by the government of Carthage, returned to North Africa with fifteen thousand troops. Hannibal and Scipio met in 202 at Zama in the final battle of the war. Hannibal was defeated, and Rome was the supreme power in the Mediterranean.

Hannibal spent his final years as a politician in Carthage, but he became unpopular and was forced to flee to Ephesus, a Greek city in modern-day Turkey, where he poisoned himself rather than be handed over to the Romans.

Hatshepsut

There were six female pharaohs in Egyptian history. Hatshepsut, who reigned from 1473 to 1458 BCE, was the third. She was the daughter of the pharaoh Tuthmosis I. She married her half brother, who became the next pharaoh, Tuthmosis II, in 1492 BCE, when their father died. Hatshepsut and Tuthmosis II had one child, a daughter named Neferure. Tuthmosis II had a son by another wife; this son was married to Neferure while still a baby.

Tuthmosis II died in 1479 BCE. His son, now Tuthmosis III, was too young to rule. When a pharaoh was too young to rule, another member of the royal family ruled for him, as regent, until he could rule alone. Hatshepsut was the perfect choice. She was the daughter of a pharaoh, the wife of a pharaoh, and the mother of Tuthmosis III's wife. However, what happened next was quite unusual.

A Female Pharaoh

In 1473 BCE Hatshepsut stopped ruling for Tuthmosis III. She claimed that the god Amun, whom she began to call her "father," wanted her to be the pharaoh of Egypt. Historians believe that Hatshepsut dressed as a pharaoh and even wore the false beard that Egyptian pharaohs wore. Certainly she was shown dressed in this way in some carvings and paintings, perhaps because it was the way that pharaohs had always been shown. The inscriptions on the carvings sometimes display confusion, by referring to Hatshepsut as both "he" and "she."

◀ This stone statue of Hatshepsut as pharaoh, made in about 1460 BCE, comes from her funerary temple at Deir el-Bahri. It shows Hatshepsut with a male body and a pharaoh's crown and false beard.

▶ *The funerary temple of Hatshepsut, at Deir el-Bahri, Thebes, was built to stand dramatically against the sheer cliff face.*

Trade

Hatshepsut was a strong pharaoh, and Egypt was peaceful and rich during her reign. She did not go to war with Egypt's neighbors; instead she traded with them. Egyptian grain and gold continued to be traded for turquoise from Sinai, wood from Byblos, and incense from Punt. Craft workers were encouraged to make beautiful things, and to show her power and devotion to the gods, Hatshepsut also had temples built and added to. On the walls of a chapel in her funerary temple at Deir el-Bahri, Hatshepsut had scenes carved of one of her most famous trading expeditions — a journey to Punt in about 1470 BCE.

A Mysterious End

In 1458 BCE Tuthmosis III began ruling alone. What happened to Hatshepsut is a mystery. Tuthmosis sent an army of workers around Egypt to remove all carvings, paintings, and statues of Hatshepsut as a pharaoh. Only a few survived. He did not dare remove her obelisks in the temple of Amun in case it made Amun angry. So he built walls around them instead. It is not known how Hatshepsut died nor where she was buried, although she had built herself a tomb in the Valley of the Kings.

THE FOLLOWING IS PART OF AN INSCRIPTION ON AN OBELISK HATSHEPSUT HAD MADE FOR HER "FATHER," THE GOD AMUN, IN ABOUT 1465 BCE:

The king himself [Hatshepsut] erected two great obelisks to her father, Amun-Ra, in front of the chief hall, covered with much electrum. This is what Amun, lord of Egypt, said to his daughter Hatshepsut. "I gave you kingship of Egypt, with millions of years on the throne of Horus, with stability like Ra."

SEE ALSO

• Amun • Egypt • Egyptian Mythology
• Valley of the Kings

Health, Medicine, and Disease

People have always suffered from illness, disease, and injury and, from the earliest times, have sought to find cures and treatments. For many thousands of years, magic more often than medicine was used to heal people. Over time, greater knowledge of the human body and how it works led to practical solutions, especially in the ancient civilizations of the Egyptians, Greeks, Romans, and Chinese.

Ancient Egypt

The ancient Egyptians believed that the human body was born in a healthy state and could not fall ill or die except through some influence from outside the human body. They did not understand the origin of health problems or bacteria. As a result, they believed that many health problems inside the body were the work of evil forces, magic, or punishment handed down from the gods. Ancient Egyptian medical men and women, who were often priests or worked with priests, used a mixture of practical medicine and spells and charms to remove or neutralize the evil forces.

Despite their reliance on magic and gods, the ancient Egyptians made many remarkable advances in medicine. They are believed to be the first civilization to have a specialized medical profession, made up of both male and female doctors. From 2700 BCE and possibly earlier, medical schools taught Egyptian physicians how to set broken bones, to check the health of teeth and gums, and to mix a large number of medicines to help cure coughs, skin complaints, and fevers. They were also able to perform certain surgical operations, such as lancing a boil or abcess using a flint knife or a reed. Egyptian doctors were famous throughout the ancient world for their skills.

▼ Charms, such as this eye of Horus amulet, were worn by ancient Egyptians in the belief that they would bless the wearer with strength and good health.

Ancient Greeks

Medicine was still mixed with magic and religion in the ancient Greek civilization; the sick and ill often visited temples dedicated to Asclepius, the Greek god of healing, where they would perform certain rituals, including carefully washing themselves and offering sacrifices, in order to rid themselves of illness or injury.

The Greek philosopher Hippocrates (c. 460–377 BCE) was one of the first to question magical cures. Hippocrates considered medicine a science and taught that every disease had a natural, not a magical or religious cause. Hippocrates' teachings and writings influenced not only the ancient Greeks but the Romans and other civilizations as well.

The Romans

Building on knowledge from the ancient Greeks and Egyptians, the Romans schooled their physicians in scientific and religious methods. From the first century CE, a form of health service was organized, whereby doctors treated the poor for free in return for not having to pay taxes.

A number of Roman physicians learned to perform operations in army camps and gladiator schools, where serious injuries were common. Roman doctors produced hollow artificial legs and arms using sheets of bronze wrapped around a wooden form shaped like a human limb. Surgery was performed without modern pain-removing anesthetics. The most a patient could hope for was plenty of wine to help deaden the pain.

Roman doctors took on some extremely difficult operations, from setting bones and amputating arms or legs to even performing eye surgery. They removed eye cataracts, which cloud the lens of the eye and cause blurring of a person's sight, by using a fine needle inside a tube. The tube was placed in the lens of the eye and the needle used to break up the cataract, which was then sucked out through the tube.

DOCTORS' NOTES

Knowledge of ancient Egyptian medicine comes from many sources, including carvings on temples and tombs and the writings of an ancient Greek traveler to Egypt named Herodotus. The most important sources are a large number of medical texts written by scribes on papyrus. Two of the most famous texts were acquired by Edwin Smith and George Ebers.

Acquired by the German writer and Egyptologist George Maurice Ebers in 1872, the Ebers papyrus is a scroll twelve inches (30 cm) wide and over sixty-four feet (20 m) long. It contains 876 different recipes to aid or cure a huge range of diseases, from eye and facial problems to skin conditions and problems with sexual organs. The Ebers papyrus also describes the position of the heart and how it is the source of blood vessels.

The Edwin Smith papyrus is named after the American dealer in artifacts who bought the document in Luxor, Egypt, in 1862. It was written between 1600 and 1700 BCE but appears to have been copied from a more ancient document, not recovered, that dates from a thousand years earlier. Measuring over fifteen feet (4.5 m) long, the Edwin Smith papyrus describes forty-eight cases of wounds or injuries to the head, neck, shoulders, and chest. Similar to modern medical notations, the papyrus text lists the diagnosis of the symptoms of a problem followed by the treatment and the likely outcome, known as the prognosis. Among its cases are detailed treatments for many different fractures and broken bones. Some experts believe that this knowledge could have been obtained only from a place where accidents were very frequent, such as a pyramid building site. Indeed, recent studies of the bones of pyramid builders show evidence of fractures having been set and amputations completed successfully.

▶ A section of the Chester Beatty Medical Papyrus, housed in the British Museum in London. Dating from 1200 BCE, the text contains remedies and magical incantations to cure headaches and other ailments.

CLAUDIUS GALEN *129–216 CE*

Galen was a Greek physician who worked at a Roman gladiator school and then became an important doctor in the court of the Roman emperor Marcus Aurelius. Galen dissected animals to study anatomy. He discovered the importance of the spinal cord, which muscles are responsible for breathing and the human voice, that blood moves through the body, and how urine is produced in the kidneys. His detailed descriptions of human anatomy influenced doctors for a millennium.

Ancient Chinese Medicine

The ancient Chinese used massage and herbal remedies to cure many health problems. Many hundreds of preparations were created using raw materials found in nature. The roots, seeds, leaves, and flowers of many different plants were used to treat a large range of health problems. Ginseng root, for example, was used to treat dizzy spells, while the Chinese yam was believed to help cure exhaustion.

Acupuncture

The ancient Chinese believed that all human beings were made up of two kinds of energy, yin and yang, which traveled around the body along with blood. If yin and yang were kept in balance, a person would remain healthy. Acupuncture was an important way of restoring energy balance. This practice involves piercing a patient's body in certain places with fine needles in order to open blocked channels of energy. The ancient Chinese believed that the balanced and flowing energy would relieve pain and cure health problems.

SEE ALSO

- China • Chinese Philosophy • Egypt
- Egyptian Mythology • Greek Philosophy
- Hygiene and Sanitation • Marcus Aurelius
- Roman Philosophy
- Roman Republic and Empire

▶ *Two early Greek pioneers of medicine, Claudius Galen (129–216 CE) and Hippocrates (c. 460– c. 377 BCE), are portrayed in this fresco found in the church of Anagni in western central Italy.*

Hebrews

Hebrews is the earliest name of the people later known as Israelites and then Jews. The changes in their name reflect their changing fortunes as a people. Politically they were always weak and at the mercy of one neighboring empire after another. Yet they had a greater impact on history than almost all these empires, because of their religious ideas. Their belief in one God led to three world religions — Judaism, Christianity, and Islam.

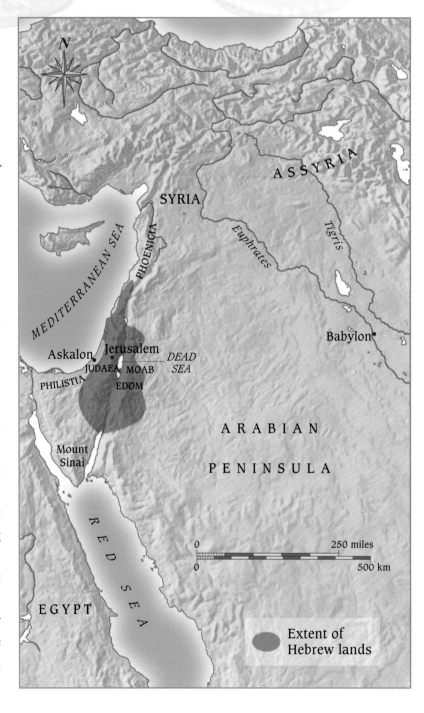

▼ The extent of the Hebrew territories.

Early History

The Hebrews' recorded traditions of their earliest history are in Genesis, the first book of the Bible. They trace their origins to a man called Abraham, who was thought to have come from Ur in Mesopotamia (modern-day Iraq). Abraham was a nomad who traveled with his family and flocks of sheep to the land of Palestine in Canaan, the place that would later be the Hebrew homeland.

Abraham's grandson, Jacob, was given a new name, Israel, which means "one who struggles with God." Israel was believed to have had twelve sons who each founded a tribe; the Hebrews lived in twelve Israelite tribes for much of their early history.

At some point, perhaps in the thirteenth century BCE, some of the tribes are thought to have settled in Egypt, where they were forced to work for the pharaoh. They were freed thanks to Moses, a great leader and teacher, who led them back to Canaan. This escape from Egypt was later called the Exodus, a Greek word meaning "the way out."

When the Hebrews reached Canaan, it was already home to many other tribes. Little by little, the Hebrews fought for control of the land of Canaan. They were led in these wars by tribal leaders called judges.

◄ This fifteenth-century Italian painting shows a fanciful view of Jerusalem at the time of Solomon, with the temple towers at the rear. Christian artists of the Renaissance were inspired by the Hebrew stories, but they had no idea what Jerusalem looked like.

Many modern historians and archaeologists question whether these early traditions of the arrival in Canaan have any factual basis. One theory is that the Israelite tribes gradually emerged from within Canaanite society. The story that they were foreign invaders may well have been a later invention to explain their differences from the other peoples around them.

Kings

In the eleventh century BCE a powerful new enemy, the Philistines, who came from the coastal plain of Palestine, moved into Canaan. Under Philistine pressure the northern Israelite tribes chose their first king, Saul. He was succeeded by David, the most famous Israelite king, who united all the tribes and conquered the city of Jerusalem and made it his capital. David's son Solomon ruled over a united kingdom and built a temple in Jerusalem.

On Solomon's death the kingdom split into two: Israel in the north and Judah in the south. Around 722 BCE the northern kingdom was conquered by the Assyrians, and the northern tribes were deported to Mesopotamia and disappeared from history. Judah alone remained, and the remaining Israelites came to be called Jews.

In 597 BCE Judah was attacked by the Babylonians. The Babylonian king, Nebuchadrezzar II, seized ten thousand captives and took them away to Babylon. Ten years later he attacked Jerusalem again, completely destroyed the city and its temple, and took even more Jews into Babylonian captivity.

HEBREWS

Note: many of the dates, particularly for the earlier periods, are disputed.

C. THIRTEENTH CENTURY BCE

Possible date of Moses and the Exodus from Egypt.

c. 1200–1050 BCE

Israelite tribes, led by leaders called judges, conquer much of the land of Canaan.

c. 1005–c. 965 BCE

Reign of David, who unites all the tribes and conquers Jerusalem.

c. 931 BCE

The kingdom splits in two, with Israel in the north and Judah in the south.

c. 722 BCE

Assyrians destroy the northern kingdom of Israel.

c. 587 BCE

Babylonians sack Jerusalem and deport many of the Jews to Babylon.

c. 536 BCE

Persians conquer Babylon and allow the Jews to return home.

323 BCE

Establishment of Greek kingdoms that rule Palestine: the Seleucids of Syria and the Ptolemies of Egypt.

160–63 BCE

Rule by Maccabean priest-kings. Rival sects form in Judaism – the Sadduccees and the Pharisees.

63 BCE

The Romans conquer Palestine.

6 BCE

Romans take direct control of the province of Judaea.

66–70 CE

First Jewish revolt.

132–135 CE

Second Jewish revolt.

▼ A representation of Ezekiel, painted in 1510 on the ceiling of the Sistine Chapel in Rome, by the Italian artist Michelangelo.

EZEKIEL

Ezekiel was a leading priest and one of the first group of Jews taken to Babylon in 597 BCE. In exile he began to have a series of powerful visions, which are described in the Book of Ezekiel. Ezekiel's early visions warned of further disasters waiting for the Jews as a punishment for worshiping other gods. The destruction of Jerusalem seemed to fulfil Ezekiel's prophecies. His later visions offered comfort to the exiles, as he explained that God would give them another chance: "A new heart I will give you . . . I will put my spirit within you and make you follow my laws. . . . Then you shall live in the land that I gave to your ancestors, and you shall be my people, and I will be your God" (Ezekiel 36: 26–28 [KJV]).

Unlike the earlier tribes who disappeared into Mesopotamia, the exiles in Babylon maintained their Jewish identity. They were held together by a series of religious leaders called prophets who explained that the people's suffering was due to their earlier failure to obey God's laws. If they would only keep the Jewish law, God would give them back their homeland.

After the Exile

When Babylon was conquered by the Persians, the Jews were allowed to return home and rebuild their temple. They traveled back to Jerusalem in waves between 538 and 520 BCE. Yet, apart from one brief period, they never again enjoyed true political independence.

One empire followed another, and the Jews had many different rulers. In 332 BCE the Persians were conquered by Alexander the Great, whose successors established Hellenistic, or Greek, kingdoms in Egypt and Syria, which ruled Palestine in turn.

Jews stood out in the Hellenistic kingdoms because of their refusal to assimilate, that is, adapt to the culture of those who ruled them. They would not worship other gods or religious images and followed strict laws controlling what they could eat.

◄ This fifteenth-century book depicts the Maccabees rising in rebellion against the Greek ruler Antiochus IV. As in all medieval art, the figures are wearing clothing of the artist's own time.

The Greek ruler of Syria, Antiochus IV, wanted to force the Jews to be like the rest of his subjects. He banned Jewish worship and rededicated the Jerusalem temple to the Greek god Zeus, whose statue he placed there. This hostile act led to a successful Jewish uprising, led by a priestly family called the Maccabees. The Maccabees, or Hasmoneans, established a new Jewish state ruled by priest-kings.

Roman Rule

Jewish independence was finally ended when the Roman general Pompey conquered Palestine in 63 BCE. For a time the Romans ruled through a dynasty of Jewish puppet kings, the most important of whom was Herod the Great, who reigned from 37 to 4 BCE. Herod was hated by his Jewish subjects, despite his attempt to win popularity by rebuilding the Jerusalem temple on a grand scale.

In 6 CE Palestine came under direct Roman rule as the province of Judaea. Roman emperors expected their subjects to pay them divine honors as a sign of loyalty. In 66 CE Jewish discontent led to a great uprising against Rome. The rebellion was crushed three years later. After a long siege Jerusalem was taken. The temple was burned and its treasures taken to Rome in a triumphal procession.

A second Jewish revolt in 132 CE was provoked by the emperor Hadrian's decree banning circumcision. Led by Shimon Bar Kokhba, the Jewish rebels held out for three and a half years against overwhelming odds. Following his final victory, Hadrian turned Jerusalem into a Roman city, renamed Aelia Capitolina, with a temple of Jupiter on the site of the Jewish temple. So many Jews were enslaved that the price of a slave fell to that of a horse.

Diaspora

The Jews survived because they were already scattered throughout the Roman Empire and beyond, living in the communities of the diaspora, a Greek word meaning "scattering." Here they continued to maintain their separate identity. As they remembered their earlier exiles in Egypt and Babylon, they continued to hope for a messiah, or "anointed one," to restore their lost kingdom.

DIO CASSIUS, THE ROMAN HISTORIAN, DESCRIBED THE DEVASTATION FOLLOWING THE SECOND JEWISH REVOLT:

Five hundred and eighty thousand men were killed in the various raids and battles, and the number of those who perished by famine, disease, and fire was past finding out. Thus nearly the whole of Judaea was made desolate.

DIO CASSIUS, ROMAN HISTORY, C. 220 CE

▲ A silver coin issued by Shimon Bar Kokhba, leader of the second Jewish revolt against Rome. One side shows the temple and the name Shimon. The other shows a lulav, a ceremonial palm branch used in blessings. The Hebrew text says, "For the freedom of Jerusalem."

SEE ALSO

Herculaneum

When Mount Vesuvius, a volcano in the south of Italy, erupted in 79 CE, several Roman towns were destroyed. Among them was the coastal resort of Herculaneum.

History of Herculaneum

The town of Herculaneum was built on the edge of the Bay of Naples in the eighth century BCE. It may have been founded by settlers from Greece who established an overseas colony there. According to another theory, it was founded by the Samnites, who were the local people in this part of Italy at that time. What is clear is that the Romans took control of Herculaneum in 89 BCE, along with Pompeii, a neighboring town. By the middle of the first century CE, the town's population had increased to an estimated five thousand people. Unlike Pompeii, which relied on trade and business to prosper, Herculaneum was a quiet residential town, with houses, villas, and little industry.

Destruction of Herculaneum

In 62 CE the region of Italy in which Herculaneum lay was rocked by a major earthquake. Scientists now believe the earthquake was a sign that Mount Vesuvius, the volcano four miles (6 km) to the east of Herculaneum, was stirring. The damage was repaired, and life returned to normal. Seventeen years later, at around midday on August 24, 79, Vesuvius erupted with devastating force. A column of ash rose an estimated twenty miles (33 km) into the sky. Some twelve hours later the column collapsed, and the result was the first of many avalanches of ash, pumice, and mud. Each surge rushed down the mountain at great speed, reaching Herculaneum within four minutes.

▶ Herculaneum was built on a coast renowned for its beauty and good climate. It was close enough to Neapolis (present-day Naples) to be almost a luxurious suburb, where the wealthy went to relax by the sea.

THE VILLA OF THE PAPYRI

In the 1750s a villa probably belonging to Lucius Calpurnius Piso, father-in-law to Julius Caesar, was discovered at Herculaneum. From it came a library of 1,787 papyrus scrolls, every one charred to fragile carbon by the heat of the eruption. Early attempts at unrolling these ancient books were painfully slow: it took four years to open the first one.

There are still some 400 scrolls waiting to be unrolled, and 450 are so difficult to read that their content remains a mystery. Of those that have been read, many are works of the philosopher Philodemus of Gadara (c. 110– c. 35 BCE), written in Greek. A collection of Latin texts, perhaps containing works by Cicero, Horace, and Virgil, is thought to remain buried in the villa.

▲ Many of Herculaneum's buildings, such as this shop, have been preserved to roof height. The timber work is modern, based on an authentic Roman design.

Although many residents probably had time to escape, some did not. When archaeologists excavated the town's boat chambers, they found the skeletons of around three hundred people. Perhaps they had been sheltering in the chambers, waiting on the beach for boats to rescue them. Instead they died from the searing heat (up to 750° Fahrenheit) and lack of oxygen.

Discovery of Herculaneum

After the eruption Herculaneum completely vanished from sight. It was buried beneath one hundred feet (30 m) of debris, where it remained untouched until the 1700s. By this time a new town, Resina, had been built above the remains of Herculaneum. In 1709 a workman digging a well in Resina uncovered blocks of marble. He had dug down to Herculaneum's theater. This chance discovery led to the gradual uncovering of the ancient Roman town; around two-thirds of Herculaneum's fifty-five acres (22 hectares) have now been revealed.

SEE ALSO
• Caesar, Julius • Pompeii • Roman Republic and Empire

Herodotus

Herodotus (c. 484–424 BCE) is called the Father of History because he was one of the first to write the kind of book now called a work of history. He wrote about the people of the eastern Mediterranean, especially about the wars between the Greeks and the Persians. He called his work an "inquiry," the Greek word for which is *historia*. History is what this subject has been called ever since.

Life

Herodotus was born around 484 BCE in the Greek colony of Halicarnassus in Asia Minor (in modern-day Turkey), which was then under Persian rule. His parents were wealthy, and as a young man he became involved in politics. However, he clashed with the ruler Lygdamis and left Halicarnassus. Soon afterwards Herodotus departed on the first of his journeys around the eastern Mediterranean, during which he took notes for the history he was to write.

Travels

Herodotus traveled to Egypt and the Nile, to Tyre (present-day Lebanon), and down the Euphrates River to Babylon, in present-day Iraq. He went to Scythia, north of the Black Sea, and to Greece. For some time he lived in Athens. However, around 444 BCE he settled in the new Greek colony of Thuria in southern Italy, where it is likely he worked on his notes and where he died.

Writings

Herodotus's writings mix history, geography, and descriptions of different peoples he met. However, his methods were similar to those of a modern historian: he placed the greatest importance on firsthand sources; for example, he interviewed men who fought in the Persian wars. Of secondary importance was what he read in official court and temple documents or in long poems, such as Homer's *Iliad*. He also obtained information from the writings carved on statues and monuments and from the physical remains of the past, much as archaeologists do.

▶ This bust of Herodotus has his name carved in Greek at the base. It is a double-headed sculpture, the other head being that of Thucydides, another great historian of the fifth century BCE.

IN THIS PASSAGE HERODOTUS DESCRIBES HOW THE EGYPTIANS CAUGHT CROCODILES:

They bait the hook with a hunk of pork and let it float out into midstream, and at the same time, standing on the bank, take a live pig and beat it. The crocodile, hearing its squeals, makes a rush towards it, encounters the bait, gulps it down and is hauled out of the water. The first thing the hunter does when he has got the beast on land is to plaster its eyes with mud; this done, it is killed easily enough – but without this precaution it will give a lot of trouble.

▲ The Mausoleum at Halicarnassus, Herodotus's birthplace, was regarded as one of the Seven Wonders of the Ancient World. Built as a vast burial tomb for King Mausolus, it is an indication of the wealth that was to be found in many of the Greek colonies.

Achievement

Herodotus's work has been criticized. He has been accused of placing too much importance on Athenian sources and of not understanding military matters. There may be some truth in this argument, but for many readers Herodotus's enthusiasm about what he saw and heard is more important. He had great respect for the achievements of cultures other than that of Greece. Even the Persians, the greatest enemies of the Greeks, he praised for their justice, their love of truth, their loyalty to their king, and their courage.

SEE ALSO

• Greece, Classical

Hinduism

Hinduism is the modern Western name for India's ancient religion — or rather, religions. Hinduism includes a remarkable variety of gods, beliefs, and religious practices, all of which developed over time, as the character of the gods changed and new religious ideas were invented. Unlike other world religions, Hinduism has no single founder and no one holy book. Originally the word *Hindu* was simply the name of the people who lived beyond the Indus River.

▼ *Statues of the gods cover Hindu temple walls. This eleventh-century statue shows Agni, the ancient Aryan fire god.*

Hinduism is very tolerant of the beliefs of other religions. There is an Indian saying that there are 333 million gods, and Hindus are free to worship whichever god they please. For many Hindus, all of these gods are aspects of a single all-embracing godhead, or universal spirit, called Brahman.

Beginnings

Hinduism has been compared to an ocean with many rivers, or sources, flowing into it. One important early source was the religion of the Aryans, the people living in northern India between 1500 and 1000 BCE. Aryan religion was governed by a hereditary class of priests, called brahmans, who performed open-air animal sacrifices for a series of great gods, including Indra, the sky god, and Agni, god of fire. This practice was very different from those of later Hinduism, yet the ancient Aryan religious texts, the Vedas, are still treated as sacred by Hindus.

While Aryan priests were performing their sacrifices, the other peoples of India were worshiping a variety of local gods. Mother goddesses, ancestors, rivers, lakes, trees, and animal spirits were all worshiped. In time, as all these cults flowed into Hinduism, new gods were created.

Reincarnation

By the middle of the first millennium BCE, many Indians came to believe in reincarna-

तिन् गुणैलेत्तिन्त्र एएग्राइ गुणल्ल ग्र्र्

गुल्लैः व्फ्रु ग्ग्रण ग्र्रण त्र्मि ग्र्ल् ग्ग्र्ल् गएगि

म्ब्ल्नैद्य्ग्रैल्एल्यैव्छय्

tion, the idea that after death a person is reborn in a new body, which might be that of any living creature. Reincarnation was closely linked to what Hindus called the law of karma (action), which says that every action a person performs, whether good or bad, has a consequence in one's next life.

A person's karma would also affect his or her place in society in the next life. Indian society was divided into castes, or classes, whose members only married others from their own caste. At the bottom of Indian society were the outcastes, whom other Hindus regarded as "untouchable." Outcastes had the dirtiest jobs, such as disposing of dead bodies. During the Gupta period, untouchables were expected to bang a gong as they walked along a street, to warn respectable Hindus to avoid them.

Belief in reincarnation was used to justify the caste system: untouchables deserved their fate because of their behavior in a past life. However, if outcastes lived well, they could look forward to a better life next time around. The concept of reincarnation led to a reaction against the brahmans' animal sacrifices. To many, it seemed wrong to kill animals who might have been people in previous lives. As a result, many high-caste Hindus became vegetarians.

▲ Three couples who belong to the brahman caste, painted in 1828. Brahmans are the highest of the Hindu castes.

THIS PASSAGE FROM A RELIGIOUS TEXT OF AROUND 800 BCE EXPLAINS THE PRINCIPLE OF REINCARNATION:

Those whose behavior here is pleasing, they will have a good birth – the birth of a brahman, a kshatriya (warrior) or a vaishya (merchant). Those whose behavior here stinks, they will have the birth of a dog, a swine, or an outcaste.

CHANDOGYA UPANISHAD

Ascetism

By 500 BCE many Indians had begun to practice asceticism, or self-denial for religious reasons. Common requirements included fasting (going without food) and withdrawing from society. Ascetics also invented many ingenious ways of punishing themselves, including lying on thorns, hanging upside down from trees, and standing on one leg or raising one arm in the air for long periods.

The aim of asceticism was to free the spirit by denying the body's needs. Many Hindu ascetics wanted to unite their own atman, or spirit, with Brahman, the spirit of the universe. By doing so, they hoped to escape from the cycle of rebirth and find *moksha* (joyful release).

Gods

By the beginning of the first millennium CE, three gods had come to be seen as more powerful than all the rest. Their names were Brahma, Vishnu, and Shiva. Brahma was the creator of everything. He was often shown in art with four heads. Each head was supposed to have produced one of the four collections of Vedas. Brahma was a remote figure who did not involve himself in the world after creating it. He was never widely worshiped, and for many Hindus his position as supreme god was eventually taken over by Vishnu or Shiva.

Vishnu was the preserver and protector of the world. A friend to humanity, he was believed to come to earth whenever disaster threatened. For each appearance he would

◀ Hindu ascetics are still a common sight in India. They often sit motionless for hours, meditating.

VARANASI

For Hindus, India is a sacred land, full of holy rivers, mountains, and cities. Many places, such as Varanasi (also called Benares), are holy because they are linked with a particular god. Known as Kashi, the city of light, Varanasi is thought to have been founded by Shiva. Ever since the sixth century BCE, pilgrims have traveled in the thousands to Varanasi to wash in the sacred Ganges River. Hindus believe that if they die in Varanasi, they will achieve instant moksha.

assume a different form, called an avatar, that is, one who descends. At different times he came as a fish, a wild boar, and a turtle. His best-known avatar was the hero Krishna, who became one of India's most popular gods. Hindus told many stories about Krishna's adventures and his love of playing tricks.

While Vishnu was the preserver, Shiva was called the destroyer. His worshipers believed that he regularly destroyed the world only to recreate it again. Unlike the pleasure-loving Krishna, Shiva was a god of asceticism. In art he was sometimes shown with matted hair and a body covered in ashes, like a Hindu ascetic. Shiva was believed to sit in the Himalayas, meditating and storing up energy. He would then release this energy by dancing. As he danced, his feet were believed to smash worlds to dust.

Over time, Vishnu and Shiva were each given families of gods. Shiva's wife is Parvati, and their son is the elephant-headed god, Ganesha. Vishnu's wife is Lakshmi, goddess of prosperity.

None of these gods were represented in art until the first millennium CE. It was only under the Gupta kings (320–500 CE) that Hindus began to build temples and carve sculptures of their gods.

▼ *By dancing Shiva is thought to destroy the old universe and create a new one. This bronze statue shows him dancing inside a ring of fire, which represents destruction and rebirth.*

SEE ALSO
• Aryans • Buddhism • Gupta Empire • Indian Philosophy
• Kushan Empire • Mahabharata • Mauryan Empire • Ramayana

Hittites

The Hittites are the earliest-known speakers of an Indo-European language, a language group from which most languages of Europe, India, and Iran developed. The Hittites' main language, which is now known as Hittite, was originally called Neshite. No one knows for sure where the Hittites originated, but their language suggests that they came from eastern central Europe.

Around the start of the second millennium BCE, the people who came to be known as Hittites started migrating to the land of Hatti (hence the name Hittites) in central and eastern Anatolia, in modern-day Turkey. Gradually the Hittites became the dominant force, and by 1750 BCE they controlled most of Anatolia, which became their homeland. Hattusha, or Hattusas, was the name of their capital city (near present-day Boghazkale, formerly Boghazköy).

Wars

The Hittites were fierce warriors. They were the first people to make iron weapons, and their soldiers were highly skilled at building fortifications. These military advantages enabled the Hittites to conquer other nations and extend their empire.

During a period called the Old Kingdom, which lasted from around 1650 to 1460 BCE, the Hittites invaded the now-vanished kingdom of Arzawa in southeast Anatolia (in the north of modern-day Syria and Iraq). Around 1590 BCE the Hittite king Mursilis I sacked Babylon and removed the sacred statue of Marduk, the chief god, from its temple.

From around 1400 to 1200 BCE the Hittites enjoyed a second phase of prosperity, known as the New Kingdom, or "empire period." During this period they extended their control over Syria and thus came into conflict with the Egyptians, who wished to control the same territories.

The two sides met at the Battle of Kadesh, which took place around 1300 BCE. The Hittites, led by King Muwatallis, rode into battle on 3,500 chariots. It was the first time that wheeled vehicles had

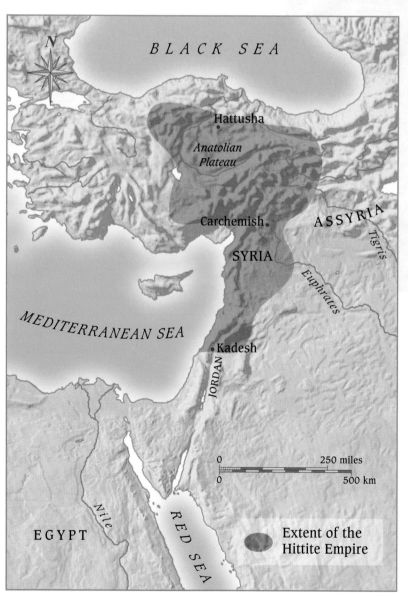

▼ *The extent of the Hittite Empire.*

BLACK SEA

N

Hattusha

Anatolian Plateau

Carchemish.

ASSYRIA

SYRIA

Tigris

Euphrates

MEDITERRANEAN SEA

• Kadesh

JORDAN

0   250 miles
0   500 km

EGYPT

Nile

RED SEA

Extent of the
Hittite Empire

been used in a war. The Egyptians, led by the pharaoh Ramses II, claimed victory, but the battle proved to be inconclusive. The Hittites would not retreat from their territories in Syria.

Sixteen years later the Egyptians were forced to sign a peace treaty with Muwatallis's successor, King Hattusilis III, and thus accepted the Hittite presence in Syria.

HITTITES

c. 1900 BCE

The Hittites invade the region known as Hatti.

c. 1800 BCE

The Hittites build the capital of Hattusha.

c. 1650–1460 BCE

Old Kingdom.

c. 1590 BCE

The Hittites conquer Babylon.

c. 1400–1200 BCE

New Kingdom.

c. 1300 BCE

The battle of Kadesh.

c. 1193 BCE

The Hittite kingdom is conquered (possibly by the Sea People).

c. 710 BCE

Remaining Hittite city-states are conquered by Assyrians.

MUWATALLIS *REIGNED C. 1320–1294 BCE*

King Muwatallis, the son of King Mursilis II, inherited his father's throne in the time of the New Kingdom. Muwatallis went to war with the pharaoh Ramses II when the Egyptians took Palestine from the Hittites and moved the border between the two powers to the Orontes River in Syria. During the Hittite defense of the city of Kadesh, Muwatallis gave the impression that he and his armies were in the far north of his kingdom. The Egyptian armies walked into the trap; they marched toward Kadesh and straight into the enemy. After a bloody battle the Egyptians retreated. Muwatallis was proclaimed the savior of the Hittite nation. He moved from his palace in Hattusha to Dattassa, a city closer to the border with Egypt. From there he could keep watch on the pharaoh's movements.

▼ This relief, carved around 1294 BCE, shows Ramses II's army attacking the Hittites during the Battle of Kadesh. As it was made by Egyptians, it shows the pharaoh's army routing the Hittites. In fact, the Egyptians may have lost the battle. The relief can still be seen in the temple at Karnak.

Government

The Hittites were ruled by an all-powerful king. He was the military leader of the nation, its chief priest, and its supreme judge. People considered the king to be the spokesman of the gods. When he died, he was proclaimed a god himself.

The king was the owner of all the land ruled by the Hittites, tracts of which he leased out to feudal lords who also served in the army. Provincial governors looked after the interests of the king in the various provinces of the kingdom. Other states in the outer reaches of the empire were ruled by puppet kings. They followed strict rules that were outlined in treaties signed by the Hittite king.

Culture and Law

The Hittites were a powerful military force, but their culture was not very strong, and they tended to absorb the beliefs and ways of life of people they conquered. Following their sack of Babylon, the Hittites adopted the Babylonian way of life. However, they made one important modification to Babylonian culture: they adopted a milder form of the law code of the Babylonian king Hammurabi.

The Hittites were more merciful than other cultures of their age. Under Hammurabi's law code, even petty crimes, such as getting drunk in public, were often punishable by death. The Hittites reserved capital punishment for only a handful of serious offenses, such as violent attacks against lords and kings. Even the punishment for the murder of a common citizen was often just a heavy fine.

Religion

The Hittites believed in a great number of gods, many of whom were worshiped under different names in different regions of their empire. Their chief deity was the storm god. This god was known by a variety of names, including Tarhun, Taru, and Teshub.

People also worshiped the sun goddess, originally called the goddess of Arinna, after the city where her cult began. She was also addressed as Arinnitti and Wurusemu. The sun goddess of Arinna was believed to look after the empire and bring it wealth and prosperity. The Hittite king and queen were her high priest and priestess. The sun goddess had three children: Nerik, the

▶ *This bas-relief sculpture shows Taru, the Hittite god of the weather. It formed part of a stele, a large stone column covered in images and inscriptions, found in Babylon.*

eldest, was also a weather god. His sisters were named Mezzulla and Hulla.

By the late thirteenth century BCE the family of the storm god and the sun goddess had become the most important gods of the Hittites.

The End of the Hittites

Because of the great size of the Hittite empire, its rulers had to struggle to keep its borders safe from invaders. Nor could they always quell uprisings among their conquered subjects. Around 1193 BCE the Hittite Empire was destroyed by unknown invaders. It has been suggested that these invaders were the mysterious Sea People. No one is certain who the Sea People were, but they might have been pirates and invaders from Greece, Crete, and Sicily.

Some Hittite territories that survived ruled themselves as independent city-states. However, by 710 BCE, these last bastions of Hittite culture had been taken over by the Assyrians, who were becoming the dominant force in the region. The Hittite culture had come to an end.

SEE ALSO

- Assyrians
- Babylonians
- Egypt
- Ramses II

▶ *This Hittite drinking vessel was made between 1400 and 1200 BCE. It was probably used during religious ceremonies. Some sacred drinking cups also had a frieze around the rim depicting gods and rituals.*

Hopewell Culture

The Hopewell people settled in what is now southern Ohio between around 300 BCE and 450 CE. Evidence of these people – including burial mounds and earthworks that were formed in precisely shaped circles, squares, and octagons – has been found in or near what is now the Scioto River valley. The Hopewell culture, which developed from the earlier Adena culture, was responsible for creating a variety of mound-building sites across a large area of the territory known as the Eastern Woodlands.

Knowledge of this remarkable culture originated in the eighteenth century, though its name derives from a late-nineteenth-century landowner named Hopewell, whose property covered an area where these people had lived two thousand years earlier. Originally, archaeologists believed that the finely crafted jewelry and carvings they found on Hopewell's land and elsewhere in the region must have been the work of much more recent inhabitants.

Origins

The origins of the Hopewell people are not known for certain. They were one of several peoples that settled in what is now the eastern United States. Some historians believe they came there from the northeast. Most evidence, however, suggests they moved up from the south. Remains of similar civilizations have been found in the Mississippi River valley. The people formed a variety of local cultures, each with its own style of craft and jewelry. Trading between the settlements bound the people together and formed the culture.

Food and Farming

Buried deep in the ground at the Hopeton Earthworks are the remains of deer, fish, shells, bones, antlers, and animal hides. From this evidence it is clear that the Hopewell people were hunters. They also grew a lot of their own crops. A grass called goosefoot yielded seeds that could be

▼ Sites of the Adena and Hopewell cultures.

Adena heartland
Hopewell area of influence
Adena site
Ohio Hopewell site
Hopewell site

N

Great Lakes

Squawkie Hill

Trempaleau

Miamisburg
Adena
Newark
Grave Creek Mound
Mound City

Marietta
Harness

Havana
Fort Ancient
Turner
Criel Mound

Serpent Mound
Hopewell
Seip

Ohio River
Adena Park
Tremper
Portsmouth

Crab Orchard

Tennessee River

Mississippi River

Miller

ATLANTIC OCEAN

Porter

Marksville

Gulf of Mexico

0   500 miles
0   800 km

ASTRONOMY

It is likely that the Hopewell people studied the sun, moon, and stars. The geometric exactness of their circles, squares, and octagons may be connected with the precise measurements they made of the moon's phases: its waxing and waning over each twenty-eight-day month and also the time and place on the horizon of its rising and setting.

A circle-and-octagon enclosure at Newark, Ohio, is very similar to another one at High Bank, Chillicothe, over sixty miles (97 km) away, and is linked in a straight line by a set of parallel walls. Scholars believe the sites mark the extreme northern and southern rising points of the moon.

HOPEWELL CULTURE

c. 1000 BCE

Adena culture of northeast flourishes.

c. 300 BCE

First evidence of Hopewell people in Scioto valley.

c. 200 BCE

Sites at High Bank, Hopeton, and Seip date from this time.

c. 100 BCE

Newark earthworks develop; culture grows.

c. 200 CE

Height of Hopewell people's activity, in building, astronomy, and religious ritual.

c. 300 CE

Many new buildings are begun; there are also signs of Hopewell people dispersing and moving on.

c. 450 CE

Evidence that people have left the area; sites are emptying or declining.

crushed into flour or mixed with water to make a paste. Hopewell people also grew sunflowers (for their seeds) and barley and may have learned to grow maize from travelers who moved up from the south.

▶ A Hopewell culture carving of a kneeling man. The knot on his forehead could be a single horn, the symbol of a shaman (holy man).

Buildings

The outlines of buildings have been traced, and some of the circles and patterns are very precise. What remains appears to consist mainly of walls and burial mounds or large open spaces for celebration or worship. Very little is known about the houses in which Hopewell people lived. Homesteads by the Scioto River contain features such as meeting places, heaths for fires, and community rubbish dumps.

▶ *This pot, decorated with relief carvings of severed hands, was probably used in connection with Hopewell death cults and ceremonies.*

SEE ALSO
• Art
• Death and Burial
• Religion
• Technology

Arts and Crafts

Archaeologists believe the Hopewell people were traders who bought and sold artifacts from distant places. They wore ceremonial costumes decorated with pearls and seashells from the Gulf of Mexico and with human bones. They also made decorated clay pots and carved sharp tools and blades out of a stone called obsidian. Carved copper falcons and plates, mica carvings, and fossil ivory decorations have all been found close to human bones. When someone died, precious objects and gifts were buried alongside the body, perhaps for the journey to the next life.

Religion and Death Rituals

The burial mounds and geometric open spaces suggest that celebration, worship, and ritual were important to the Hopewell people. When a person died, a great ceremony was carried out. They cremated bodies in specially made clay-lined basins and built burial mounds to commemorate the dead. The nature of Hopewell religion or their god or gods is not known.

CALEB ATWATER, AN EARLY EXPLORER OF HOPEWELL MOUNDS IN OHIO, WROTE IN 1800:

What surprised me is the exact manner in which they had laid down their circle and square.... The measurement was more correct than it would have been ... had the present inhabitants undertaken to construct such a work.

Houses and Homes

Along with food and water, shelter is a basic human need. From the earliest times, people sought out shelter to protect themselves from the cold, from the rain and snow, from wild animals, and from other unfriendly people.

Nomads and Cave Dwellers

The earliest peoples moved from place to place in search of food and had no permanent homes. Instead, these nomadic peoples sought out naturally occurring shelter in caves, rocky outcrops, and forests and woodland. Caves were warmer, drier, and safer than outside, and also shelter from the wind made fires easier to light. Out in the open, simple tents made of branches and covered in the hides of animals acted as shelters. People learned how to sew hides together and roll them up to take their shelter with them when they moved. Gradually, as people learned how to grow plants and rear animals for food, they settled in one place and built longer-lasting homes.

Celtic Homes

The ancient Celts, who lived in small family groups known as *fines*, are an early European people who built permanent homes. Most Celtic homes were round and had relatively low walls made of materials that were easily found in their home area. The materials were either stones piled high into rough walls or branches and twigs woven together and covered in mud. The roof was made from a simple frame of tree branches covered with bundles of tied straw from nearby fields or, in some highland areas, with heather. A Celtic home tended not to have windows, and the doorway was often left as a gap or covered with an animal skin hung over the opening.

▼ *This round thatched house (left) and smaller rectangular outbuildings are part of a reconstruction of an ancient Celtic village found near Quin in Ireland. The wooden frame in the foreground is used to hang and dry out animal carcasses.*

The interior of a Celtic house was dark and smoky, with some but not all of the smoke from the central fire rising out through the roof. The Celts did not have much furniture. They squatted or sat on animal furs and cushions on the floor. In winter the Celts often kept some of their animals inside the house with them.

Stone and Brick Homes

Many early civilizations used the same sorts of raw materials as the Celts to build similar kinds of home. Over time some civilizations learned how to make bricks by pressing mud into wooden molds and leaving the mud to dry out in the sun. The houses in the 7000-BCE town of Çatal Hüyük (in modern-day Turkey) were built out of a timber frame filled with mud bricks. There were no streets or front doors in Çatal Hüyük; all the houses were built adjoined to each other, and the entrance was through the flat roof. Archaeologists believe this unusual design was for protection from wild animals and hostile peoples.

Rich and Poor Homes

As civilizations developed and settlements became larger, the differences between rich and poor became apparent in the types of homes people chose to live in. In ancient China, for example, the poor often lived in simple timber-framed huts covered with a simple form of plaster made from mud, with a thatched roof of straw and grasses. This basic design remained unchanged for

MAYAN HUTS

The Maya in Central America lived in huts made either from stone walls, in highland areas, or from rough planks of wood, in rain forest areas. A Mayan house consisted of one rectangular room with rounded corners, no windows, and one central door facing east. Sometimes there was another door that led to a second hut, used as both a kitchen and a chicken coop. In the kitchen, women would cook on a grill set over three rocks.

Roofs were made of thatched grasses or large palm leaves. The roof was usually steeply angled to let the heavy tropical rains run off. The Maya had no nails, so all of the joints in the home were tied together with a flexible but strong type of tropical vine called a liana. The floor in a Mayan home was made of sascab, *a foundation of gravel covered with white packed soil.*

many centuries. Wealthier Chinese lived in magnificent stone and brick buildings featuring a large wall that enclosed many rooms and often courtyards and a garden. Inside the living quarters, clay stoves provided heat, while windows were covered with either stiff paper or hemp sacking. The walls were often tiled and decorated with artistic silk wall hangings. Wealthy ancient Chinese houses often contained many pieces of low-lying furniture as well as beautiful woven rugs and mats.

In ancient Egypt, only tombs and temples were made of stone. Houses were made from mud brick, which in Egypt's hot, dry climate lasted a long time. Even royalty lived in palaces of mud brick, although they were plastered and decorated with beautiful painted scenes and inlaid tiles and had splendid furniture.

◀ A scene from the Book of the Dead shows the house (right) of an ancient Egyptian scribe Nakht and his wife Tjuiu, who was a priestess. The pool (left) is surrounded by trees and date palms. The house is raised on a mudbrick platform.

ROMAN CENTRAL HEATING

The Romans developed a system of heating that was built under the floor and behind the walls. Called a hypocaust, it was found in bathhouses and in larger Roman homes. One or all of the ground-floor rooms were supported on stacks of clay tiles, with a closed basement area about two feet (60 cm) deep beneath the floor. This area was filled with hot air from a furnace built outside the house. Draughts carried the heated air through the basement area. As the hot air rose, it warmed the floors of the rooms and also traveled up vertical channels in the walls, called flues, and thus heated the walls of the rooms.

Hypocausts were found only in the houses of the very wealthy, as the system required regular maintenance. Slaves or household workers used a long-handled pole to rake out the ashes and push new fuel into the fire. The fire was mainly fueled by small branches and twigs placed two to three feet (60–90 cm) into the furnace's opening.

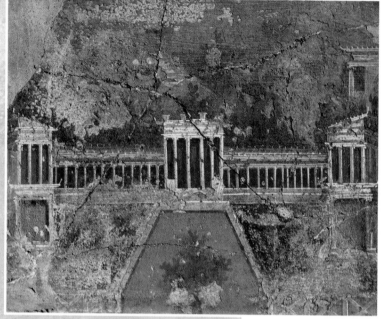

▲ This fresco from Pompeii shows the kind of elaborate many-columned architecture used in a Roman villa of around 45 CE.

Roman Housing

There were different types of housing in the Roman Empire as well. The poor lived in cramped apartments in low structures that were called *insulae*. The ground floors of *insulae* were built of brick or stone, but the floors above were made of wood and were often unsafe. Fires, disease, and collapsing *insulae* buildings were quite common in ancient Rome.

For wealthy Romans, however, there were no such problems. They lived either in a spacious town house called a *domus* or out in the countryside in a large house called a villa. Roman villas were often built of bricks held together by mortar, which the Romans made by mixing sand, lime, and water. They added stone chippings to create a form of concrete.

SEE ALSO

• Çatal Hüyük • Celts • China • Cities • Hygiene and Sanitation
• Maya • Palaces • Roman Republic and Empire • Technology

Huangdi

Huangdi (also spelled Huang-ti) is the Yellow Emperor of Chinese legend. He is said to have ruled China about 4,500 years ago. He and his wife, the empress Lei Zu, were said to have taught the Chinese people many new skills, including how to make pottery and weave silk. In ancient China, Huangdi was honored as a god.

In China written records date back to around 1500 BCE. Prior to this time was a mysterious era when heavenly beings were said to have lived on earth. One of the most famous was Huangdi, who legend said ruled China for a century. The first of five emperors who helped humans to make new discoveries, Huangdi was the greatest of them all.

▼ A portrait of the Yellow Emperor, Huangdi. According to legend, after living on earth for a century, Huangdi rose to heaven mounted on a dragon.

Son of Heaven

Huangdi is called a "son of heaven." He owned a dragon, which he rode across the sky. He was the mighty warrior who fought seventy battles to unite the Chinese empire. He then appointed four princes to rule China under him.

On the banks of the Yellow River in northeast China, Huangdi taught his people many new skills, including how to make boats and wheeled vehicles. He showed people how to build houses and fine palaces. He gave them armor and demonstrated how to make pottery. His wife, Lei Zu, showed the people how to cultivate mulberry trees and weave silk.

Huangdi was a great patron of arts and sciences, including medicine and mathematics. He allowed one of his chief ministers, Cang Jie, to teach people how to write. Other ministers introduced the calendar, mathematics, and musical instruments to the Chinese people. After reigning for a hundred years, Huangdi ascended to the heavens and was never seen again.

HUANGDI'S SECRETS

Chinese legends say Huangdi "possessed the essence of thunder." Like Zeus of Greek mythology, Huangdi was a storm god whose main weapon was the thunderbolt. When his minister Cang Jie showed people the secret of writing, the sources say "all spirits cried in agony, as the innermost secrets of nature were revealed."

▶ This bone, dating from the time of the Shang kings (around 1500 BCE), bears the earliest-known example of Chinese writing — one of the gifts of Huangdi to his people, according to legend. Such bones were used in religious ceremonies to look into the future.

Origins of the Legend

The legend of Huangdi may have been based on the life of a real chieftain who ruled northeast China in prehistory. As the stories of this chieftain were passed down through the ages, Huangdi was elevated to the status of a god. The Chinese were one of many civilizations that gave divine beings credit for the development of skills such as writing and farming.

Chinese civilization began around five thousand years ago in the region around the Yellow River, where Huangdi is said to have lived. Before that time, early Chinese people had lived as nomads, hunting animals and gathering wild food. In about 3000 BCE, however, people began to settle on the banks of the Yellow River. They grew crops in the fertile soil, kept animals, and made pottery.

According to various legends, the first great line of kings in China was called the Xia, but there are no written records of its existence. The first records date back to the time of the Shang kings, who ruled northeast China from the 1760s to 1122 BCE. Archaeological finds have proved that the Shang already possessed many of the skills that Huangdi was said to have taught humans. As well as knowing how to write, the people of that era could make fine pottery, build palaces, and forge bronze tools and weapons, and they went to war in horse-drawn chariots.

SEE ALSO
• China

Huns

The Huns' contribution to history was brief and very violent. In the course of just one hundred years, these fearsome horsemen from western Asia swept through large parts of Europe and caused great damage to the Roman Empire.

Origins

Historians cannot be sure exactly where the Huns came from. As a nomadic people, they did not necessarily stem from a single homeland. It is also difficult to be certain what race the Huns were or what language they spoke, because they absorbed many characteristics of the European tribes they conquered.

However, it is almost certain that they were Asian. They entered Europe from somewhere beyond the Caspian Sea. Some historians associate the Huns with the Xionghu, a tribe that attacked China during the Han dynasty (206 BCE–220 CE). If the historians are correct, the Huns' journey to the Danube is even more extraordinary.

Almost all of what is known about the Huns comes from two Roman historians. The first was Ammianus Marcellinus (330–395 CE). He describes the Huns as wild, both in their appearance and in their habits. Their diet was simple, consisting of meat, roots, and edible plants. According to Marcellinus, the Huns did not cook their meat with fire but rather by sitting on it as they rode their horses. The Hunnish tribes roamed in bands. They were ruled by military chieftains and had no overall king.

The second historical account was written in 448 CE by Priscus. By this time, according to Priscus, the Hunnish lifestyle had been influenced by contact with surrounding tribes and with the Roman Empire.

◀ This map shows the extent of the Huns' kingdom at the time of the Battle of Châlons. They conquered and destroyed large parts of the Roman Empire.

The Huns terrified everyone who met them. This painting of the Huns riding into battle dates from 1891.

By the time of Priscus, most Huns were ruled by a single king. Attila (reigned 434–453), their greatest king, handpicked the men who would govern his vast empire for him. The Huns had become practiced in the art of negotiation. They would ride out to meet Roman generals and other barbarian kings to negotiate hostage swaps, protection payments, or the terms of war.

The Extension of Power

The people of Europe first became aware of the Huns around 370, when they crossed the Volga River. Within ten years the Huns were setting up camp on the banks of the Danube River in modern-day Hungary. They had marched across 1,250 miles (2,000 km) of rivers and mountains and stood at the edge of the Eastern Roman Empire.

The Huns remained in what is now Hungary for around fifty years. During that time, expanding north and west, they established dominion over many of the Germanic tribes of central Europe. Their kingdom grew in size, until it stretched from the Alps to the Baltic in the north and to the Black Sea in the east.

The Huns were also involved in several border skirmishes with the Eastern Roman Empire. However, from 420, the Roman Empire paid Rugila, the Hunnish king, to protect their border from marauding barbarian tribes.

Attila's Battles

In 441 the Romans stopped their payments to the Huns. Led by Rugila's nephew Attila, the Huns swept over the border. Over the next eight years, they went on a murderous rampage through the Eastern Roman Empire. They destroyed city after city, slaughtering thousands of Roman soldiers and citizens. In desperation the emperor Theodosius II agreed to pay the money he owed and a lot more besides.

The following year Attila launched a daring invasion of Gaul (present-day France). At the Battle of Châlons, he suffered the only military defeat of his career. The Huns withdrew and set their sights on Italy.

MASTERS OF THE ART OF WAR

Mounted on warhorses, the Huns charged back and forth across large areas of Europe. They destroyed city after city and killed anyone who stood in their way. They would scale enemy ramparts without warning and destroyed camps before the enemy knew they were being attacked.

In battle the Huns did not use any standard formation. Instead they rode chaotically around the battlefield, scattering and regathering at great speed, a tactic that terrified their enemies. They were highly skilled archers. Their arrowheads were made from sharpened bone, and they rained them on the enemy from a distance. In close combat the Huns would throw nets over enemy swordsmen, who would become so entangled they could not move.

The Huns marched south, destroying cities as they went. However, for no clear reason, they turned back before attacking Rome. There are several theories to explain this change of heart: Attila's forces were severely weakened after Châlons; there was a famine in Italy; and the Huns' base, by the Danube, was under attack. According to another story, Attila saw a vision of Saint Peter, who warned the Hunnish king that he would die if he attacked Rome. However, no one can say for certain why the Huns withdrew.

HUNS

370–376 CE

Huns march from Caspian Sea to Danube; they defeat Alans and Goths.

434 CE

Attila becomes king.

441–449 CE

Devastation of the Balkan provinces of the Eastern Roman Empire.

451 CE

The Huns are defeated by Aetius and his allies at Châlons.

452 CE

Huns invade Italy, but stop short of Rome.

453 CE

Death of Attila; his sons become kings and fight among themselves.

455 CE

Huns defeated in Pannonia.

▼ *A gold coin with a portrait of Emperor Theodosius II. Attila defeated his armies and forced the Roman Empire to pay the Huns 1,980 pounds (900 kg) of gold a year.*

▲ This painting by Raphael depicts the defining moment in 452 when the Huns were about to invade Rome. Pope Leo I rode over the mountains on a white horse and into the Huns' camp. According to legend, Attila saw a vision of Saint Peter above the Pope's head and for the only time in his life, he was afraid.

AETIUS 396–454 CE

Aetius is often called "the last of the Romans." He was a noble and cultured man, as well as a brilliant general who fought many battles in defense of the Roman Empire. However, by 476, twenty years after his death, the Roman Empire in the west had collapsed.

As a youth, Aetius had spent some time as a hostage of the Huns. This experience may have helped him in his later confrontation with them. At the Battle of Châlons in 451, Aetius commanded the first army to defeat the Huns.

Disintegration

When Attila died, two years later, the Huns quickly faded as a power. Attila's kingdom was divided between his sons, who immediately started fighting against each other. The Huns' enemies saw their opportunity, and in 455 a barbarian force led by the Ostrogoths defeated the Huns in Pannonia (present-day Hungary). It appears that the Huns then blended into other tribes. They are never mentioned again as a separate people.

SEE ALSO

• Attila

• Goths

• Roman Republic and Empire

Hunting and Fishing

During the Paleolithic and Mesolithic eras (Old and Middle Stone Ages), from 2.5 million years BCE to 5800 BCE, all societies lived as hunter-gatherers. They survived by hunting animals and gathering wild vegetables, fruits, nuts, and berries.

Stone Age Hunters

Because they required a fairly constant supply of meat, Stone Age people followed herds of animals. Thus, the movement of these people was based on the migrating activities of the animals they hunted. During the main hunting seasons of spring and autumn, hunters would live in temporary camps, always ready to pack up and move on. However, they may have lived in permanent bases during the less active summer and winter months.

Winter was often a difficult time for Stone Age hunters, who had to find shelter from the cold weather and enough food to see them through until spring. Caves often provided convenient shelters in highland areas. In lowland regions, such as the Ukraine, remains of houses have been found made of mammoth bones. There is also evidence that portable tents with poles and animal skins were used.

Weapons and Tools

Stone Age people developed a wide range of weapons for hunting. Ax heads, spearheads, and arrowheads have been found, as well as hammers, knives, and scrapers. Weapons and tools were generally made from stone, usually flint, although sometimes bone was used. Handles for axes, knives, and launchers were made from wood, but hardly any of these have survived.

When an animal was killed, very little of its carcass was wasted. Bones were used for tools and weapons, and internal organs were used for vessels and twine. The discovery of awls (piercing tools) and pins and needles suggest that animal skins were sewn together to make clothing, tents, and sacks for carrying possessions from place to place.

▼ This ironstone hand ax, found in South Africa, is around 600,000 years old. Although called hand axes, they were probably used as all-purpose tools for cutting, digging, and trimming. It is possible that some had wooden handles, but no handles have survived.

Hunting Methods

Animals could be picked off individually by bands of hunters, but before the onset of winter, mass kills were required. Herds of animals, such as bison, were stampeded over the edge of a cliff. The animals were either killed outright by the fall or were finished off with spears and arrows at the foot of the cliff. Teams then moved in to butcher the carcasses for their meat and skins. The remains of these hunts have been found on the plains of North America.

Fishing

Rivers, lakes, and seas have provided people with sources of food for many thousands of years. Stone Age harpoons, made of bone,

suggest that hunters from that era waded into shallow water to spear fish. The jagged edges of these harpoons prevented the fish from slipping off the point. Fishhooks made from bone, stone, and thorns, dating back five thousand years, were found in a cave at Skipshelleren in Norway. Huge rubbish heaps called middens, dating from the Mesolithic period (c. 8300–c. 5800 BCE) and containing thousands of shells, have been found in many different parts of the world and offer proof that shellfish was very popular in Stone Age times. Long cylindrical stones called limpet hammers were used to prise shellfish off rocks.

Fishing nets made out of vines were also developed during the Mesolithic era, and with nets came the use of boats, which enabled fishermen to catch large numbers of fish in one trawl. Communities bordering the great oceans hunted whales and other sea mammals during this period, especially on the west coast of North America and the west coast deserts of what is now Chile and Peru. Here the earliest settlers, dating back to around 8000 BCE, are known as the Chinchorro, the local word for "fishing net," since these earliest inhabitants did not farm but lived off seafood they caught in the Pacific Ocean.

The End of the Hunter-Gatherer

With the introduction of agriculture about eight thousand years ago, the hunting and gathering way of life gradually died out. However, fishing continued as an important and nutritious supplement to the diet, especially in winter.

Although the nature of hunting changed, it remained important as a supplement to farmed produce. In Jericho, for example, gazelles were hunted long after agriculture was established.

▼ In many societies fishing has continued to be an essential source of food. This mosaic, showing men fishing with nets in Imperial Roman times, comes from the catacombs of Hadrumetum, in Tunisia.

HUNTER-GATHERER ART

Cave paintings dating back nearly 15,000 years to the hunter-gatherer era have been found in southwest France and northern Spain. On the walls of many limestone caves are colorful paintings of bison, deer, lions, aurochs (wild oxen), horses, and mammoths. Careful examination has shown that the artists first scraped the shape of the animal into the rock with a stone or piece of bone and then outlined it in charcoal. The paint, made from ground rocks mixed with water or fat, was colored from pigments found within the caves. Iron oxides could provide yellow, red, and brown paint, while charcoal could be used for black. The paint was applied with the fingers or with animal skins. At Altamira in Spain, a ceiling painting sixty feet (18 m) long and thirty feet (9 m) wide, depicts twenty-two animals, mainly bison, almost life size. It could be that these animals, so important for the survival of early man, were being honored.

▲ *One of the bison from the Altamira cave in Spain. As they seem to have been painted in deliberately inaccessible places within the cave, perhaps they were visited only occasionally, for special ceremonies or rituals.*

Hunting also became important as a social activity. Neolithic (New Stone Age) sites contain the remains of dogs that accompanied hunting groups, dating from around 10,000 BCE. In ancient Greece and Rome, men joined in the hunt, especially when on horseback, as part of their military training. As societies came to be dominated by powerful elites, hunting provided an opportunity for chiefs and leaders to impress their subjects with their prowess at killing wild animals.

SEE ALSO
- Art • Jericho
- Prehistory

Hygiene and Sanitation

With the coming of agriculture came villages, settlements, and by the fourth and third millennia BCE, towns and cities. With large numbers of people living closely in a small area, problems arose, such as how to deal with large amounts of sewage safely. It was also necessary to supply the inhabitants of these communities with a regular and clean water supply.

Drainage

The Indus valley civilization (2500–1500 BCE) pioneered a very good drainage system, especially at Mohenjo Daro, in present-day Pakistan. Many of the streets of this city, which had a population of nearly 40,000 people, had drains constructed with baked bricks under them. The contents of the Great Bath in the citadel and individual domestic lavatories emptied into them. In case of blockages, manholes were constructed at regular intervals to allow access.

When the Etruscans ruled Rome in the sixth century BCE, they attempted to drain a marshy low-lying area for the construction of the forum. Around 570 BCE they succeeded by building the Cloaca Maxima (Great Drain), which converted a stream encased by a solid stone tunnel into a main drain that still runs into the Tiber River.

▼ With such a big population, Mohenjo Daro, in modern-day Pakistan, had to deal with large amounts of sewage. The water from the Great Bath helped wash the waste from people's homes out of the town. The brick-lined drains can be seen here.

There also exist the remains of drainage systems from ancient Egypt: the shower room of king Ramses III in his palace beside the temple of Medinet Habu dates back to around 1170 BCE.

Water Supply

The most common form of water supply was the well. Wells were square or circular shafts dug as deep as the water table and then lined with either wood or stone. Wells were adequate but could easily be polluted by objects falling into them or could dry up in long periods of arid weather.

One of the earliest attempts to provide a clean and safe water supply was made by the Greeks on the island of Samos in about 530 BCE. A tunnel 6.5 feet (2 m) square, cut through limestone, was designed by Eupalinos of Megara to link the town of Pythagoria with a clean spring half a mile away. Herodotus, the Greek historian, who lived in Samos for a while, called it "one of the wonders of the world." The water was piped into the town and was still in use until late in the Roman period.

THIS WITTY ACCOUNT BY THE WRITER SENECA SHOWS THAT THE PUBLIC BATHS OF ROME WERE FAR MORE THAN JUST PLACES TO WASH; THEY WERE SOCIAL CENTERS TOO.

I'm in the middle of a roaring racket. My lodgings are over the baths! Imagine every possible outcry to shatter your eardrums. When the more athletic bathers swing their dumbells I can hear them grunt as they strain, or pretend to and hissing and gasping as they expel their breath after holding it. There's a lazy chap happy with a cheap massage: I hear the smack of the hand on his shoulders. . . . Now add the argumentative pickpocket caught in the act and a . . . man who loves the sound of his own voice in the bath. After that, the people who jump into the pool with an almighty splash. . . . The attendant . . . never silent except when making somebody else scream by plucking hair from his armpits. There the refreshment man with his wide range of cries, the sausage vendor, the confectioner . . . each with his own vendor's cry.

SENECA, FIRST CENTURY CE

▶ *The Great Bath, at Aquae Sulis (present-day Bath, in southwest England), built by the Romans in the late first century CE. It was the center of a large complex of rooms that were served by the naturally hot water from a nearby spring. The floor of the bath was lined with large sheets of lead.*

Bathing

Roman towns and cities required large quantities of water every day in order to supply the communal bathhouses, or *thermae*, that were the mark of Roman civilization. The Greeks had used hot air and steam baths in the fifth century BCE, which the Romans copied. However, with the invention of the hypocaust, a system that heated rooms and walls with dry heat, public bathhouses developed into large complexes of hot and cold rooms with plunge baths. They were relatively cheap to run and soon became an important part of Roman social life.

In 350 CE Rome had nine public baths, all demanding vast supplies of water. Design and layout varied, but most had a changing room, a *frigidarium* (cold room with cold plunge), a *tepidarium* (warm room), and a *caldarium* (hot room with hot plunge bath). They also provided other facilities, such as a gymnasium, a bowling alley, libraries, and lecture theaters. The baths at Caracalla in Rome even had a sunbathing lounge conveniently facing the southwest so that its customers could catch the afternoon sun.

Sewers

In ancient Rome, underground sewers, often running beneath the streets, were constructed of stone or wood and took away the water from bathhouses and toilets. The public toilets, or *foricae*, were built over sewers, with either wooden or stone seats, and were communal — there were no cubicles. Overflows from public fountains and street gutters also linked up with the sewers. The destination of all this waste was usually the nearby river. Roman writers complained about the foul state of some sections of the Tiber, especially in the summer.

Despite these efforts to clean up towns and cities, disease was still rampant in built-up areas. Streams and rivers were polluted with sewage, which was a source of bacteria, and "fevers" brought on by infection were very common in damp, marshy, and poorly

PERSONAL HYGIENE

The people of ancient Egypt liked to keep themselves clean. They washed after rising and both before and after the main meals. For soap they used a mineral called natron or sometimes a cleansing cream made from powdered lime mixed with vegetable oil. For mouthwash they used natron salt, chewed herbs, or used a specially prepared breath freshener made from myrrh, a scented resin.

Only the wealthiest Egyptians had their own bathrooms. Most cleaned themselves by washing from a basin or by a dip in a canal or the Nile River. By Greek times there were public bathhouses, which archaeologists have excavated at Tebtunis in Egypt, the oldest dating to the third century BCE. They contained showers, stone basins, and a stove to heat the water.

The Greek historian Herodotus recorded that the priests had to bathe twice a day and twice a night and shave their entire bodies every other day to remain free of lice and keep themselves clean and pure.

▲ A bronze Egyptian razor dating from around 1450 BCE. The curved handle allowed for a steady grip during shaving.

drained regions. One of the biggest threats came in the form of the plague. It hit Rome on many occasions, most seriously in 71 CE and again in 166 CE, when the plague swept across the whole of the western Empire. The cause was believed to be infection by troops returning from the East. The disease hit both rich and poor, and in 251 CE it even claimed the life of the emperor, Hostilian.

SEE ALSO
• Aqueducts • Greece, Classical • Health, Medicine, and Disease • Herodotus • Houses and Homes • Mohenjo Daro • Palaces • Rome, City of

Iliad and Odyssey

The *Iliad* and the *Odyssey* are ancient Greek epics, long poetic tales of heroic deeds. The author of these works is traditionally regarded as the poet Homer. The stories were not invented by Homer but were based on popular myths and legends. When the poems were written there was already a tradition of bards telling the two stories.

The *Iliad* and the *Odyssey* were composed in the late eighth century BCE but set earlier, perhaps in the twelfth century, a time when men were thought more heroic than in the author's own time. The *Iliad* is about the ten-year Trojan War. The *Odyssey* tells the story of one Greek hero, Odysseus, returning from that war.

The *Iliad*

The Trojan War began with the Trojan prince Paris falling in love with the beautiful Helen, wife of Menelaus of Sparta, and carrying her off to Troy. Menelaus, calling on other Greek kings to help him get her back and avenge this dishonor, gathered a huge army and sailed east to Troy.

▶ A marble bust of the poet Homer. Little is known about Homer, and his poems may even have been written by two different poets. However, there is a tradition that he was blind.

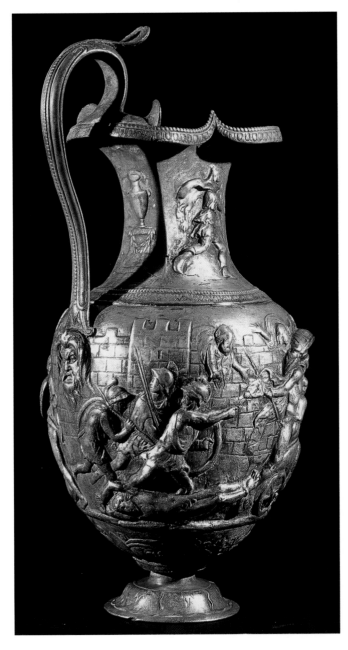

The *Odyssey*

The *Odyssey* begins in Odysseus's house in Ithaca. Odysseus is assumed to be dead. His wife, Penelope, is being wooed by impatient and rowdy suitors. Odysseus's son, Telemachus, is powerless to get rid of them. Penelope promises to choose a husband when she has finished her weaving, but every night she unravels what she has done. Inspired by the goddess Athena, Telemachus sets off in search of his father. He learns that Odysseus is being held captive by the nymph Calypso.

The story switches to the trials of Odysseus. Calypso lets him go, and he is washed up on the shores of an island. He tells the earlier part of his story to the island's king, Alcinous. Odysseus describes the warlike Ciconians, the drugged lotus eaters, the one-eyed Cyclops, and the witch Circe, who turns men into pigs. He has even visited Hades and talked to the dead. He has also survived the sweet-voiced but deadly sirens and the monster Scylla and the whirlpool Charybdis.

◄ *A silver Roman vase, made between the first and third centuries CE, showing Achilles dragging the body of Hector around the walls of Troy.*

The story of the *Iliad* focuses on the greatest Greek hero, Achilles. He kills hundreds of Trojans every day. However, when his slave girl, Briseis, is taken from him by the Greek commander Agamemnon, Achilles is outraged and withdraws from the battle. The Greeks start to suffer heavy losses, so Achilles allows his friend Patroclus to lead his forces.

When the Trojan prince Hector kills Patroclus, Achilles is grief stricken. In despair and fury he returns to the battle and kills Hector and then drags his body around the city behind his chariot. The poem ends after Achilles takes pity on Hector's father and lets him reclaim his son's body.

HECTOR FIGHTS BRAVELY UNTIL CONFRONTED BY ACHILLES OUTSIDE THE GATES OF TROY:

Fear struck Hector as he beheld him. He dared not stay where he was but fled in dismay from before the gates, while Achilles darted after him at top speed. Like a mountain falcon, swiftest of birds, that swoops down on a frightened dove – the dove flies before him but the falcon with a shrill scream follows close after, determined to have her – even so did Achilles pursue Hector with all his strength, while Hector fled under the Trojan wall as fast as his legs could carry him.

ILIAD, BOOK 22

ODYSSEUS AND HIS MEN ARE IMPRISONED IN THE CAVE OF A ONE-EYED MONSTER, POLYPHEMUS THE CYCLOPS. ODYSSEUS HAS GIVEN HIS NAME AS NOBODY. THE CYCLOPS JOKES THAT HE WILL EAT NOBODY LAST. WHEN ODYSSEUS BLINDS HIM, THE MONSTER'S CRIES BRING HIS BROTHERS TO THE CAVE MOUTH:

"What on earth is wrong, Polyphemus? Why are you disturbing the quiet night and our sleep with this shouting? Is a robber stealing your sheep? Is someone trying to kill you by treachery or violence?"

Out from the cave came Polyphemus's great voice: "O my friends, Nobody's treachery, Nobody's violence, is killing me."

"Well then," they answered, in a tone that settled the matter, "If nobody is assaulting you, you must be sick. Sickness comes from great Zeus and can't be helped. All you can do is pray to your father, the god Poseidon."

And off they went.

ODYSSEY, BOOK 9

Finally Odysseus reaches home alone. He disguises himself as a beggar but eventually reveals himself to Telemachus. Together they destroy the suitors. Odysseus is reunited with Penelope and with his aged father, Laertes.

Comparisons

There are notable differences between the two epics. There are no villains in the *Iliad*, and it contains a strong sense of fate. Nor are there any fantastic monsters. The *Odyssey* is divided into separate episodes. Odysseus faces many challenges and confronts strange monsters and evildoers who get what they deserve. Odysseus is a new kind of hero, who uses trickery as well as strength and bravery.

The ancient Greeks and Romans assumed that Homer wrote both poems. Modern scholars have suggested that the *Odyssey* was written by a second poet a little later, although the styles are similar.

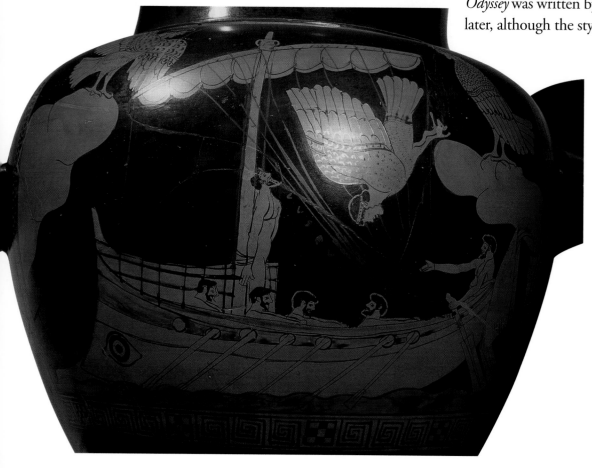

 A vase painting showing Odysseus tied to the mast of his ship at his own request so that he can hear the song of the Sirens without being enchanted into staying with them forever.

SEE ALSO

- Agamemnon
- Greek Mythology
- Mycenaean Civilization
- Mythology
- Odysseus • Troy

Indian Philosophy

Philosophy is a Greek word meaning "love of wisdom." Although the Greeks are usually thought of as the inventors of philosophy, India has an even older philosophical tradition. Like the Greeks, the early Indian philosophers asked the big questions of life, such as "What is reality?" and "Who am I?" and the most important question of all, "How should we live?" Indian philosophy has always been seen as having a practical purpose, as a guide to life.

Throughout India's history, philosophy has been bound up with religion; many of the most sacred ancient books asked philosophical questions. A good example is the Creation Hymn in the Rig Veda, written more than three thousand years ago (Vedas comprise the entire body of Hindu sacred writings). Unlike the Bible's confident opening, "In the beginning God created the heaven and the earth," the Indian hymn is full of doubt: "Where this world has come from, perhaps it formed itself, or perhaps it did not. The one who looks down on it, in the highest heaven, only he knows — or perhaps he does not know."

Upanishads

Indian philosophy really begins with the Upanishads (that is, "sessions" or "teachings"), a group of religious texts dating from around 900 to 500 BCE. These accounts, in prose and verse, of the teachings of gurus (teachers) contain many different ideas about life. One idea is that the world, which is one of constant change, is an illusion, hiding a deeper unchanging reality. The goal of life is to see through illusions to a deeper truth, to find a way of uniting the atman (individual soul) with the brahman (unchanging soul of the universe).

◀ *Brahma, attended by a devotee, holds a page of the Vedas.*

Six Schools

Over the years, the Upanishads were interpreted in different ways; as a result, six philosophical schools, or *darshanas* (viewpoints), developed. Each taught different ideas and practiced different techniques. One common characteristic was the use of short, memorable sentences, called sutras (threads), to help people remember the teachings.

Samkhya (which means "counting") is the oldest school, founded by Kapila in the seventh century BCE. The school taught that all things come from two separate principles, Praktri (matter), which is always changing, and Purusa (person), which is unchanging.

Vaisheshika ("individual characteristics"), developed by Kanada in the third century BCE, was an attempt to work out the structure of reality. Kanada said that everything in the universe is composed of nine basic substances: earth, water, fire, air, ether, space, time, self, and mind.

Nyaya ("analysis") was founded by Aksapadama Gautama in the second century BCE. Nyaya and Vaishesika had similar teachings, but Nyaya stressed clear thinking and logical argument as ways to see through the world of illusion.

Yoga ("union"), created by Patanjali in the third century BCE, was a system of mental and physical discipline using meditation, breath control, and posture to free the mind.

Mimamsa ("inquiry"), developed by Jaimini in the second century BCE, was the school least concerned with finding new

◄ *A nineteenth-century painting of Kapila, founder of the Samkhya school of philosophy. He sits in the lotus position, with his feet drawn up over his thighs. This was, and still is, a common position for meditation. It keeps the body in a fixed but also relaxed state and thus frees the mind.*

▼ *A follower of yoga, from an eighteenth-century series showing yoga techniques. Like Kapila, he is sitting in the lotus position.*

ideas. Instead, it used the Vedas, the ancient hymns, as well as the Upanishads, to work out religious rituals and proper ways of behavior.

Vedanta ("end of the Vedas") was also closely based on both the Vedas and Upanishads. Its most influential teacher, Shankara (788–820 CE), elaborated on the Upanishad idea that there is only one reality. All distinctions, such as those made by the Vaisheshika school, are due to ignorance, or maya. One finds freedom by removing this ignorance. Vedanta has been the most influential school and is still followed by many Hindus.

Charvaka

Charvaka, a philosopher who lived around 600 CE, disagreed with all the other schools. His philosophical tradition was not based on the Upanishads. He claimed that the physical world is all that exists. There is no deeper hidden meaning and no afterlife. He said people should make sure they enjoy themselves in this life. The school he founded was called both Charvaka and Lokayota ("worldliness").

Charvaka's school did not last, probably because it was so opposed to most ancient Indian thinking. All that is known about Charvaka comes from books written by his enemies.

▲ *This painting, from around 1400, shows the birth of Mahavira, founder of the Jain religion and philosophy.*

Two New Religions

In the sixth century BCE another tradition led to two new philosophies, Buddhism and Jainism, which developed into religions. Each is concerned with how the way one lives affects one's fate after death.

Buddha taught that everything, including the self, is subject to change. The important thing is that the person change for the better. The goal of life is to escape from the cycle of suffering and rebirth and reach nirvana, a state of nothingness and peace.

Mahavira, the most important founder of Jainism, taught that the soul is unchanging but that bad behavior attracts karma, a substance, like dust, that weighs the soul down. A person should aim to shed karma by acting in an unselfish way. Mahavira's central idea was that people must avoid harming any other living thing.

SEE ALSO
- Alexander the Great • Aryans • Ashoka • Buddhism
- Greek Philosophy • Hinduism • Ramayana

ACCORDING TO THE GREEK HISTORIAN ARRIAN, WHEN ALEXANDER THE GREAT INVADED INDIA IN 327 BCE, HE MET A GROUP OF INDIAN PHILOSOPHERS CALLED GYMNOSOPHISTS (NAKED WISE MEN). ALEXANDER, WHO HAD BEEN TAUGHT BY THE GREAT GREEK PHILOSOPHER ARISTOTLE, WAS EAGER TO LEARN FROM THEM. ARRIAN DESCRIBED THEIR MEETING.

On the appearance of Alexander and his army, these men stamped with their feet and gave no other sign of interest. Alexander asked them through interpreters what they meant by this odd behavior, and they replied: "King Alexander, every man can possess only so much of the earth's surface as this we are standing on. You are only human like the rest of us, except you are always busy and up to no good, traveling so many miles from your home, a nuisance to yourself and to others. You will soon be dead, and then you will own just enough earth to bury you under."

ARRIAN, *ANABASIS*, SECOND CENTURY CE

Glossary

anesthetic A drug, gas, or other method of deadening all or part of the body so that it cannot feel pain.

asceticism Self-denial for religious reasons.

auroch A long-horned wild ox, now extinct, but thought to be an ancestor of modern domestic cattle.

bard Poet who recited long poems from memory, usually accompanied by music.

cult A system of religious or spiritual beliefs.

Egyptologist Someone who studies the history and artifacts of ancient Egypt.

electrum A mixture of gold and silver that was seen by the ancient Egyptians as the most precious metal.

fossil ivory The ancient remains of the teeth or tusks of animals.

funerary temple A temple built near the tomb of a dead person where prayers and offerings could be made.

Hades In Greek mythology, the underworld kingdom inhabited by the souls of the dead.

Horus In Egyptian mythology, a sky god who represented kingship and was usually shown as having a falcon's head. Horus was the son of Isis and Osiris.

Islam The religion of Muslims, based upon the teachings of Muhammad, who lived during the seventh century CE.

legionary A Roman soldier who belonged to a force of around 5,500 men, called a legion. He served in the army for between twenty and twenty-five years.

lyre A plucked string instrument used in ancient Greece.

moksha In Hinduism, a release from the cycle of death and rebirth.

mortar A sticky mixture of sand, water, and cement used to attach bricks to one another.

myrrh A pleasant-smelling gum obtained from various trees in Africa and southern Asia; it is used in perfume, incense, and medicinal preparations.

natron A white, yellow, or gray mineral once used in embalming and as a soap.

nomadic Referring to people that move from place to place seasonally in search of pasture for their herds or food and water.

nymph A minor goddess or spirit of nature in mythology, a nymph inhabited areas of natural beauty, such as woods, mountains, and rivers, and was traditionally regarded as a beautiful young woman.

obelisk A tall, square-based column with a pyramid shape at the top.

papyrus A kind of reed that grew by rivers and in marshes in ancient Egypt. The stems of the reeds were beaten flat and laid over each other to make a smooth sheet that could be written upon and rolled up for storage.

pumice A light, porous rock formed from solidified lava.

Punic Wars Three wars fought between Rome and Carthage to decide which of them should be the supreme power in the Mediterranean. They spanned a 118-year period, with the third and final conflict ending in 146 BCE with the destruction of the city of Carthage.

Punt Ancient Egyptian name for a part of Africa not certainly identified but probably the coast of present-day Somalia.

Sinai A peninsula in northeastern Egypt.

terra-cotta Unglazed reddish-brown hard-baked clay, often used to make pottery objects.

tribute Payment made by one state or tribe to another as a sign of submission.

writing tablet A small, thin sheet of wood used for carrying a written message. One type of tablet was coated with wax onto which a message was scratched with a metal writing instrument called a stylus. Because the stylus scratched through the wax, it cut into the wood below and left an impression that could be read. Another type of tablet was uncoated; a reed pen was used to write directly onto it with ink.

Index

Page numbers in **boldface type** refer to main articles.
Page numbers in *italic type* refer to illustrations.